Jackson's Call to Greatness

Snapshots of how World War II touched our lives

An old combat ship escorts an Army Air Force plane over Germany. This photo was taken by Staff Sgt. Philip J Lee, who served as a B-24 bomber tailgunner.

All inquiries should be addressed to:
Editorial Department
Jackson Citizen Patriot
214 S. Jackson St.
Jackson, MI 49201

Printed in the United States

ISBN 978-0-9815030-1-1

Table of contents

Leaving home

Dorothy Hoyt, back left, and Mary Kennedy, front center, check out Navy recruiting information in the Consumers Power Co. building on W. Michigan Avenue. The women did not join the WAVES.

A Selective Service letter, dated Sept. 21, 1942, instructs Edwin Lester Wright to report to the local draft board for induction into the Army. Early draftees left from the Hayes Hotel, but later it was changed to the sixth floor of the National Bank building, now the County Tower building. From there, it was down E. Michigan Avenue to the Michigan Central Railroad depot, where they boarded for basic training.

Frederick Hammond kisses his mother, Ethel Hammond, goodbye at the Michigan Central Railroad depot. Hammond was among the first contingent of Army draftees from Jackson.

Raymond Lavern "Red" Brunk carries a 1-A classification on his draft card from the Selective Service. Brunk later entered the Marines and was a private first class, serving in the South Pacific on Tinian Island.

The United States, a nation of immigrants, found itself frightened and fractured in 1939 as mother countries around the world toppled into war.

But any questions of whether to fight, and on whose side, were blasted away on Dec. 7, 1941, by a surprise Japanese attack on Pearl Harbor.

In one intense hours-long attack, the United States lost two battleships, a destroyer, a minelayer, and 188 airplanes. Six battleships, three cruisers and a destroyer were damaged. Some 2,388 were killed, and 1,178 were wounded.

Because of its unique posture as a power in both the Atlantic and Pacific oceans, the United States was obliged to fight two wars — one in Europe and Africa and the other in the Pacific, each requiring tremendous outlays ➡

Clark Equipment Co. issues Duane Huntoon a separation agreement from Frost Gear & Forge so he can enter the service. Huntoon served in the Army as a Tech. 5.

Family and friends of Ethel Mae "Nancy" Fillhart, second right, give her a send-off May 30, 1945, at the Michigan Central Railroad depot. Fillhart trained at Ottumwa Air Base in Iowa and became a seaman first class.

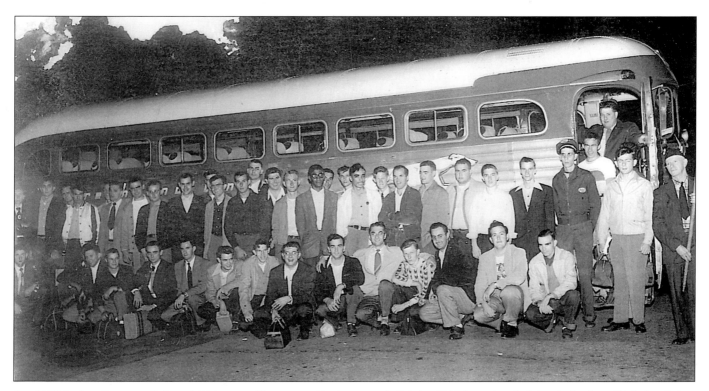

Arnold Waltz, kneeling seventh from right, leaves with a group of Jackson men in October 1944 for various training destinations. Waltz headed to Maritime Services boot camp at Sheepshead Bay, Brooklyn, N.Y. He became a Merchant Marine quartermaster, serving on the fuel tanker Tuolumne Meadows.

Training

Army Pfc. Fred Smith points out the Fort Custer sign. The Battle Creek installation was the site of Smith's basic training.

Pvt. Wendell W. Phillips, front row, second from right, completes Army basic training in 1942 at Fort Custer in Battle Creek.

of manpower, ships, airplanes, ammunition and the other implements of war. The United States lined up with the Allies — Great Britain, France, the Soviet Union, Canada and China, among others — against the main Axis powers — Germany, Italy and Japan.

Within months, America, a nation isolated and unsure of its role, was transformed into the arsenal of democracy and wielder of the most potent fighting force the world has ever known.

Twelve million men and women served in the military during roughly 44 months of war. Area residents joined the fray, fighting all around the globe. Virtually every other American had their back, manufacturing, growing, processing, rationing, saving and praying to bring the troops home.

Less than a month after Pearl

Pvt. Arnold Garred, middle row standing, fourth from right, lines up after basic training at Fort Custer in Battle Creek. Garred shipped out to the Army Air Corps in April 1943.

Harbor, Gen. Douglas MacArthur abandoned Manila in the Philippines, falling back with his forces toward a deadly trap on the island of Corregidor at the base of the Bataan peninsula.

Americans were mightily cheered when MacArthur, one of their greatest heroes, rode a roaring PT boat through the Japanese blockade at Corregidor and escaped with his family and staff to Australia, where he took over as Supreme Commander of the Pacific.

"The primary purpose of this is the relief of the Philippines," he said in explaining his escape. "I came through and I will return."

American and Filipino defenders finally were overwhelmed at Bataan and then Corregidor, ending for good any hopes that the Philippine Islands could be saved from the Japanese.

Some 76,000 Allied soldiers, ➡

Seaman First Class Ethel Mae "Nancy" Fillhart spent her WAVE training at the Naval Air Station at Ottumwa, Iowa.

Navy WAVES from Jackson gather together during training. They are, left to right, Norma LaFave, Tura Lee Hart, Dorothy Heydlauff, Elizabeth Murgejewski and Ruth Howse.

Phillip J. Lee, front row, fifth from right, poses with his Army induction class on Jan. 1, 1943, at Fort Custer in Battle Creek. Lee rose to staff sergeant in the Army Air Corps.

Jack Campbell takes a break after marching in a parade at Camp Howze, Texas. The Army sergeant wears a body harness that enables him to carry a heavy backpack.

including 12,000 Americans, were captured by Japanese forces. About 5,000 of them would die on the notorious, 100-mile "Bataan Death March" to prisoner-of-war camps. Thousands more would die in the camps.

Then came news of a startling nature.

"U.S. Planes Assault Tokyo, Set Fires, Cover Big Area"

Sixteen B-25s, led by Lt. Col. James H. Doolittle, had taken off from the aircraft carrier USS Hornet lurking 620 miles off the Japanese coast. To illustrate the difficulty of the raid, it would be more than two years, June 15, 1944, before Allied planes were able to strike again at the Japanese homeland.

Still smarting from the loss at Corregidor, Americans learned

Above: Pfc. Clinton Abrams walks the streets of Camp Lejeune, N.C., in 1944. Abrams completed basic training with a group of Marines, made up entirely of black troops.
Right: Abrams, back row right, gathers in 1944 with other black Marines at Camp Lejeune, N.C. The Marines were segregated for training and later shipped to fight against the Japanese.

on May 8, 1942, that a huge battle had been raging in the Coral Sea northwest of Australia for four days.

It was the most unusual naval battle ever fought, one that set the pattern for most of the rest of the war.

In the Coral Sea, although dozens of ships were lost, no ship from either side ever saw or fired on an enemy ship. It was the first naval battle fought entirely by carrier-based aircraft.

Both sides claimed victory, with the United States claiming 21 Japanese ships sunk, including an aircraft carrier. The United States lost the aircraft carrier USS Lexington.

Then, in the first week of June 1942, came the battle that ➡

Pfc. Chester Leffler, left, Frank Kulling, center, and Frank Krause stand outside the Hotel Carlton in Miami Beach, Fla. The soldiers were billeted there March 26, 1944, during Army Air Corps training.

Army Staff Sgt. Larry Strickrodt "gets a lift from a Lucky Strike" during a break in a 25-mile training hike at Indiantown Gap, Pa.

Above: Army Staff Sgt. Andrew Kokocka grabs a sandwich during a training break in 1942.
Left: Troops parade along the streets of Camp Hood, Texas. Army Tech. 5 Bill Goudie was one of the soldiers passing in review.

may have won the war with the Japanese.

In one intense battle near Midway Island, U.S. forces broke the back of Japanese air power and set the stage for all of the island-hopping victories to come.

The two Pacific superpowers slugged it out with bombers and torpedo planes. There was little ship-to-ship contact.

Most of the damage was done in one six-minute attack June 4, when U.S. dive bombers caught the Japanese carriers as their flight decks were crowded with bombs and refueling planes.

Three carriers were mortally wounded and a fourth was destroyed later in the day. Over the next three days, U.S. planes hammered at the Japanese task force, scattering it across thousands of square miles of ocean. The United States lost a carrier — the Yorktown — and a destroyer. In addition to four

Philip Leathead, right, goes through his primary training for the Army Air Corps in early 1943 at Lafayette, La. Leathead later became a first lieutenant and piloted a B-24 in the Pacific Theater.

Capt. Rolland M. Smith, back row, second from left, stands with his Army Air Corps class after completing pilots school in Denver, Colo. Smith headed to China and was a "Flying Tiger."

carriers, Japan lost a cruiser and four destroyers. More important, it lost 332 aircraft and 2,500 men, among them its most experienced, battle-hardened pilots.

And America's industrial might was swelling to a crescendo. Two years later, the United States would enter the Battle of the Philippine Sea with 35 carriers, not three.

While American attention was focused on the Pacific, the war was going badly in Europe and North Africa.

Erwin Rommel, the German "Desert Fox," was promoted to field marshal after his Afrika Korps forced the British and Free French from the port of Tobruk, capturing 3,000 prisoners, 3 million food rations and 500,000 precious gallons of gasoline.

Rommel then drove into Egypt, moving to within 20 miles of British forces digging in at El Alamein.

Also in Europe, the Allies sent ➡

Lt. Col. Claude Spencer, right, joins his fellow Army Air Force pilot Ed Kreig in front of a C-46 transport cargo plane after flying school in Syracuse, N.Y. Spencer flew with the 5th Combat Cargo Squadron.

Army Air Corps pilot Floyd Doherty gets a look at the cockpit during his training in Oklahoma. Doherty later flew 35 combat missions with the 8th Air Force, 561st Bomb Squadron of the 388th Bomb Group.

Above: Army Tech. 5 John Zaborowski strings out a line at Fort Sill, Okla. He was a surveyor with the Army's Company E, 275th Infantry.
Left: Zaborowski ignores the airport warning sign at Fort Sill, Okla. Zaborowski was stationed there May 24, 1941.

flights of more than 1,000 bombers, carrying 6 million pounds of bombs, against the German industrial cities of Cologne, Essen and Bremen. They claimed devastation of the cities, claims denied by the Germans.

In August 1942, the United States went on the offensive in the Pacific with the battle for the Solomon Islands.

The fight has come to be known as the battle for Guadalcanal, one of seven tiny islands about 600 miles southeast of Australia. Fighting was intense on all of the seven.

In the Solomons, U.S. Marines tried out the amphibious assault tactics they would use at Tarawa,

1st Lt. James E. White stands proudly next to a P-47 Thunderbolt on Feb. 11, 1943, after receiving his "wings." White was assigned to the Army's 9th Air Force, 406th Fighter Group.

The Army's 119th Field Artillery, Battery D, Second Battalion, was a unit made up of mostly Jackson County men. It was originally headquartered at the Armory on N. Mechanic Street as a Michigan National Guard group, before being called up on active duty.

Sgt. John L. Weatherwax balances on an airplane propellor while working at the Army Air Corps mechanics school in Jefferson, Mo.

Saipan, Iwo Jima, Okinawa and other stepping-stone islands to the Japanese mainland.

For virtually the entire month of August there was fierce, hand-to-hand fighting, and attack and counterattack by naval forces of both sides. At Midway, U.S. and Japanese ships had never been in sight of each other. In the Solomons, fighting was at such close quarters that dueling ships actually collided.

When it was over, the United States had new naval and air bases closer to Japan and the occupied Philippines, and it had a victory over the full might ➡

Cpl. Everett C. Farr of the Army Air Corps was a lineman who maintained telephone equipment. This particular job in 1944 was in the direct line of airport traffic in Norwich, England.

and determination of the Japanese fleet.

In North Africa, the British 8th Army under Lt. Gen. Bernard Montgomery had taken the offensive, driving Rommel back from El Alamein in Egypt into Libya and toward Tunisia.

In an attempt to trap the Germans, the first U.S. forces to enter the European Theater in large numbers landed Nov. 8 at such North African ports as Casablanca and Safi in Morocco and Oran and Algiers in Algeria.

Six months later, Axis forces in North Africa surrendered to the combined U.S. and British forces. Rommel escaped to Germany, but left thousands of soldiers behind, including 16 generals.

American, British and Canadian soldiers stormed into Sicily in the early dawn hours of Saturday, July 10, 1943, opening what some described as the "Battle of Europe" against the Axis powers. Within two weeks, the capital at Palermo was captured by troops of Gen. George

Army Pfc. Donald Smith waits for his turn at rifle practice at Camp Roberts, Calif.

Major Franklin "Jim" Tilford, far left, lines up Army troops for review at Ora Bay, New Guinea.

1st Sgt. Steve Trujillo puts his Army troops through drills out in the fields of France.

S. Patton Jr., who drove 60 miles in 58 hours through collapsing Italian resistance.

By November 1943 the Axis powers appeared to be on the run in every corner of the globe.

In eastern Europe, the Red Army had regained hundreds of thousands of square miles of Russian territory, forcing the Germans back from Stalingrad to the west bank of the Dnieper River and regaining the ancient capital of Kiev.

In the final week of November, three of the largest bombing raids in history, each involving more than 1,000 heavy bombers and up to 2,500 tons of explosive, battered the German capital city of Berlin.

In the Pacific, the 75-hour fight for Tarawa, a speck of sand in the Gilbert Islands astride the equator, became known as the bloodiest in U.S. Marine history.

"Never have so many died so quickly in such a small area," according to U.S. headquarters.

The grinding war of attrition ➡

Charles Wellman, Navy special artificer optical second class, uses a sextant to determine coordinates while being stationed in Guam.

Camp Claiborn in Louisiana is one of the first stops for Kenneth Hoch, an Army private who later became sergeant.

Camp life

Cpl. Wendell W. Phillips goes through maneuvers in 1942 at the Army's Camp Robinson in Arkansas. Phillips was assigned to Company D, 58th Battalion.

Navy Petty Officer Second Class Edward R. Phelps takes his shirt off in the heat of the South Pacific. Phelps was with the Underwater Detective Operations while stationed in New Guinea, New Caledonia and the Philippines.

Army T/Sgt. Norman L. Slusser takes a break Jan. 16, 1943, while stationed in St. Augustine, Fla.

Lillian (Ovens) Campbell, seaman first class, goofs around during her time off at the Navy Air Base in Norman, Okla.

continued on every front until June 6, 1944, when electrifying news was announced by, of all people, the Germans.

American, British and Canadian troops stormed ashore in northern France, invading "Fortress Europe" in overwhelming force from sea and air.

Although pinned on the beaches for hours by withering enemy fire, Allied forces eventually moved inland, securing the overlooking bluffs so men and supplies could pour ashore.

By July 25, 1944, the armies surged through Normandy, reaching the base of the peninsula and positioning themselves to break south, chopping off the Brest peninsula, or east toward Paris.

In Eastern Europe, Russian soldiers captured Lublin and Lukow in Poland, splitting two German armies and driving to a mere 300 miles from Berlin.

In the Pacific, American Marines won the bloody battle for Saipan and poured ashore in Guam after intense shelling for 17 days.

Two nearly simultaneous events, the invasion of the Philippines on Oct. 20 and the naval Battle of Leyte Gulf on Oct. 23-26, assured that the United States would have air and naval supremacy for the rest of the war.

The Japanese fleet, its air cover destroyed in the June 1944 Battle of the Philippine Sea, was forced out of hiding by the American invasion of Leyte Island in the Philippines. In a series of four battles extending over three days, the Japanese lost 35 warships, including a carrier, three light carriers, three battleships, six heavy cruisers, four light cruisers and 12 destroyers.

Especially satisfying to the Americans was the key role played in the fight by five battleships heavily damaged in the Japanese attack on Pearl Harbor — the West Virginia, the Maryland, the Tennessee, the California and the Pennsylvania.

The great naval battle was precipitated by a U.S. invasion force of 250,000 men and more than 200 ships swarming toward Leyte, an island in the middle of the highly strategic Philippines.

Within hours of the assault, Gen. Douglas MacArthur was wading ashore through the surf and broadcasting his message to the Philippine people: "I have returned."

Meanwhile, in Europe, Allied soldiers had come up against the Siegfried Line, the massive concrete, steel and explosive defender of Germany's industrial Ruhr heartland.

Here, they found a different German soldier, one who was fighting to protect his own soil. Surrounded in the 1,100-year-old city of Aachen, a 1,500-man German garrison refused an offer to surrender, setting off a nine-day barrage of obliterating cannon fire.

The final contingent of 100 SS troops took shelter in a reinforced concrete building that was blasted apart by direct fire from 150-millimeter howitzers.

Hopes for a quick end to the war in Western Europe were shattered ➡

Army Sgt. Arthur L. Middlebrook steps out of his tent in September 1941 at Fort Shafter, Hawaii.

Friends T/Sgt. Mitchell "Mike" Skrzynski and Pvt. Paul Chmielewski enjoy a quick get-together while serving in the Army.

Army Cpl. Harold "Hal" Ziegler gets a card from special friend, Patricia Palmer, with a suggestion: "Don't flirt with the local girls." The inside of the card featured paper checkers as an alternative. Palmer also writes, "I hope you can find time for this." The game was never punched out or used.

The gear of Army Staff Sgt. Stanley Fryt is spread out for a close inspection.

Pfc. Jack Brouard tries to add a touch of home to his tent in the South Pacific. The Marine crafted the picket fence in 1944 out of shipping crates.

Army Pfc. Fred J. Smith readies his Army barrack for inspection. Smith was stationed in 1944 near New Guinea.

in December, 1944, by a fierce German counter-attack. Some 20 German divisions on Dec. 16 stormed American positions on a 50-mile front from the Monschau forest south to Trier.

By Christmas Eve, German Panzer divisions had blasted a 60-mile-deep bulge into Allied lines and given Americans their biggest scare of the war.

Even as the German spearpoint reached its farthest point west, however, Allied forces were hammering at the north and south of the bulge, narrowing its "neck" and raising the possibility of encircling and trapping the invaders.

Inside the bulge, the U.S. 101st Airborne Division at Bastogne and Army troops at St. Vith, although surrounded, were pounding at the Germans and occupying crucial road junctions.

When the bloody "Battle of the Bulge" ended on Jan. 20, 1945, the Allied lines were restored and the Germans had lost 100,000 men from their 250,000-man invasion force. Also lost were 800 tanks and 1,000 aircraft. Some 81,000 Americans and 1,400 Britons also were casualties.

On Feb. 16, some 1,500 carrier-based bombers staged a nine-hour raid on Tokyo. Newspapers said the raid was supported by "the greatest fleet ever assembled, hunting for a fight only 300 miles from Japanese shores."

On Feb. 17, U.S. soldiers and Marines stormed ashore in simultaneous raids on Corregidor in Manila Bay and on tiny Iwo

Jima, just 750 miles from Tokyo. The liberation of Corregidor opened up vast Manila Bay for use by the U.S. fleet.

Iwo Jima, eight square miles of sand, had two airfields that would allow long-range fighter planes to defend U.S. bombers all the way to Tokyo and back.

The war in Europe continued to move at a fast pace, with Germans hard-pressed to hold off the Russians from the east and the Americans, British and Canadians from the west.

On Feb. 13-15, U.S. and British bombers set off a gigantic firestorm that consumed the city of Dresden and killed between 70,000 and 130,000 people.

At the end of March 1945, U.S. tank columns were rampaging at will through the heart of Germany, thirsting for a fight with an enemy that melted away in front of their cannons.

By March 9, Bonn and Godesberg had fallen to the Allies. On March 16 the important highway linking Cologne and Frankfurt was cut; on March 20, Saarbrucken and Zweibrucken fell; on March 21, Annweiler, Neunkirchen, Neustadt and Homberg; on March 29, Frankfurt and Mannheim.

The war came to the Japanese home islands in March with devastating effect as the United States abandoned its policy of precision bombing in favor of carpet bombing.

On March 9, 300 B-29s set off a massive firestorm that burned 3,500 blocks in Tokyo. On March 16, 2,500 tons of incendiaries were ➡

Army Air Corps friends of T/Sgt. Max Hotchkin enjoy the shade on an airstrip. Members of the 115th Liaison Squadron often camped under the wings of their planes.

Walter Augustine works with Army engineers while stationed in the Aleutian Islands, Alaska.

Franklin "Jim" Tilford stands in his Army tent in 1943 near Ora Bay, New Guinea. The major ran supplies up to other areas in the South Pacific.

dropped on the shipbuilding center Kobe, setting fires that destroyed 12 square miles and were visible 100 miles away.

There was no explosion of joy when the surrender of Germany was announced on May 7, 1945.

For one thing, most people recognized that the United States still was engaged in a bloody, all-out war in the Pacific against a determined Japanese nation.

There certainly was no surprise about the surrender. It already had been announced at least 24 hours earlier — by the Germans.

Although representatives of Gen. Dwight D. Eisenhower, Supreme Allied commander, had accepted the surrender, its announcement was ordered delayed for 36 hours, until the Russians could stage a signing in Berlin.

The Supreme Headquarters, Allied Expeditionary Force, however, ordered the Germans to announce the surrender in order to stop the killing. The German announcement was spread around the world — with the Allies strangely silent about its authenticity.

As the war in Europe wound down, the war in the Pacific was reaching a feverish pitch.

Giant, U.S. B-29s, flying in fleets of 500 planes each, hit Tokyo several days in a row, leaving the city "scorched to the ground," according to returning pilots.

At Okinawa, Kamikaze "divine wind" pilots took a heavy toll on U.S. ships, and "human wave" attacks turned the battle into the bloodiest ever fought by U.S. Marines. A third

Pfc. Ray "Red" Brunk calls his tent on Tinian Island, "Sack time manor." Six Marines slept in the tent for almost one year.

Cpl. Ival Hendrick, second right, listens to Army radio communications at a Canton Island command center in the Pacific. A sign in the back provides a reminder that the airwaves were being monitored by the enemy.

of all Marines killed in World War II died in the 84-day battle.

When it ended on June 22, 87,343 Japanese were dead and only 2,565 were captured. The United States lost 9,602 dead and 15,308 wounded. Some 18 U.S. ships were sunk and 54 were damaged.

World War II ended in August 1945 with two mighty explosions that destroyed the Japanese cities of Hiroshima and Nagasaki.

The end came as a surprise to most Americans, who had been expecting a laborious and bloody invasion of the Japanese home islands, perhaps resulting in up to a million American casualties.

News that an atomic bomb had been exploded over the city of Hiroshima came on Aug. 6, just hours after the attack.

First hints of the terrible destruction came from the Japanese, who said "considerable damage" had been done by the explosion and a "considerable number" of homes had been destroyed.

Later reports by the U.S. government said 60 percent of Hiroshima, an area of 4.1 square miles, had been devastated.

On Aug. 9, a second atomic bomb destroyed Nagasaki.

Later estimates put the number of people killed in the moments of the two explosions at 220,000.

In all, 405,399 U.S. military personnel died in World War II. Only the U.S. Civil War, with 462,332 deaths on both sides, was more deadly.

World War II left an indelible mark on Jackson and the rest of the world, and its aftershocks are still being felt more than 60 years later. ★

Sgt. T/5 Albert Gaige snaps a photo of a PX (post exchange) at a camp in England.

Robert "Bubs" Richardson, Navy machinist mate third class, photographs a Christmas tree in a mess hall in Guam. The Seabee brought the tree down from the mountains with some 5th Marine Brigade motorpool men. The tree was lit using lights from old Japanese Zero planes.

Cpl. Ival Hendrick washes up in the field. Hendrick lived in a dugout on Wheeler Field on Oahu, Hawaii.

Army Pfc. Stanley Augustine stays in the sun to warm up after a shower. Augustine was in Germany at the end of the war.

Tech. 5 Dale W. Hons launders his shirt while stationed in Europe. Hons helped build 13 bridges with the Army Engineers.

Army Staff Sgt. Stanley Fryt, grabs a shave using an Army truck mirror for reflection.

Pvt. Paul Chmielewski, left, cooks up some chow in an Army kitchen.

Cpl. Louis O'Connell, back row standing fourth from left, checks out the kitchen staff of the Army officers' club on Unimak Island, Alaska. O'Connell was manager of the club, nicknamed "Louie's 'Leutian Lounge."

Above: The Army officers' mess hall in Kassell, Germany, is decorated for a Christmas meal, thanks to the efforts of Sgt. T/5 Albert Gaige.
Right: Gaige works in 1945 to feed Army troops while stationed in Kassell, Germany.

Master Sgt. Lozell Jordon, third from right sitting, knows even an Army Air Corps officer has to do his share of KP. The men were fixing a meal in 1943 in England.

Staff Sgt. Stanley Fryt, back, shares the honor of winning "Best mess hall in regiment" with one of his Army buddies.

Army Pfc. Fred J. Smith needs a new pair of pants after spending time in New Guinea. The soldier lost more than 50 pounds in 1944 because he hated the taste of K-rations.

Sgt. Elmer Syrjamaki stands near GI Joe's in Reims, France, in December 1945. The Army eating hall sign on the right states, "Soldier you are a member of the best army in the world. Show pride in it by wearing your uniform correctly."

Long lines and the extreme heat of the Mojave Desert do not stop the hunger of the 3rd Army Division during its training in 1942. Army Staff Sgt. Larry Strickrodt was in the chow line near Camp Roberts, Calif.

1st Sgt. Steve Trujillo, standing center, watches over his Army platoon while they grab some lunch. The group was making its way through France in 1944.

Army soldiers under the direction of 1st Sgt. Steve Trujillo go through the mess line. The company took a break to eat in 1944 in France.

Army Pfc. Clark Winchell gets his turn at KP duty while stationed in Hammelburg, Germany.

1st Lt. J.W. "Jay" Weeks, front right, leads his fellow Army Air Corps pilots to the chow line at the air base in Colchester, England.

Army Tech. 5 Earl Hill photographs his fellow soldiers in the mess clean-up. The front of the line gets clean rinsing; the back section suffers greasy, sudless water.

Navy Seaman First Class Lillian (Ovens) Campbell manages to smile while doing KP in 1944 at Norman Navy Air Base in Oklahoma. Campbell was assigned extra duty after coming in late one night with friends.

T/Sgt. W.B. "Pete" Caldwell grabs hold of a pet wallaby. Caldwell was in Australia in 1942, serving with the Army Air Force.

T/Sgt. Alden "Don" Lake befriends a kangaroo while serving with the Army Air Corps in Australia.

Five Jackson men from the Marine's 5th Division pose with "Mary," the platoon's mascot. From left, Cpl. Elwyn "Rabbit" Rider, Ben Fisher, Mary, Bert Shirley, Dick Hall and Jack Freeman gather in Hawaii in 1944. The dog's name came from a blind date who never showed. The dog was at the date site and followed the jilted soldier back to camp.

Army Tech. 4 Gorson R. Greening adopts a stray dog named Buddy while stationed in 1945 on Tinian Island.

Cpl. Edward Dullock tends to the horses while serving with the Army as a salvage technician in the 671st Quartermaster Salvage Collection Co.

Tech. 5 Bill Goudie hops aboard a Jeep hood with a canine buddy. Goudie was a member of Patton's 3rd Army, 97th Chemical Mortar Battalion.

Army Air Corps Tech. Sgt. Max Hotchkin shares a break with a primate friend. Hotchkin sent the picture to his family back in Concord with a note that stated, "The one with the can is the monkey."

Army Cpl. Alfred Matteson defers to the top dog, "Master Sgt. Buddy," his pet while stationed in the Philippines.

Pfc. Charles Bausano, right, sits and relaxes with two buddies and a large German shepherd while stationed in Anchorage, Alaska, on June 1, 1944. Bausano was a radio operator for the 11th Army Air Corps.

Capt. Victor E. Linden sits in the cockpit of a bomber plane. Linden served as an Army flight surgeon in France and England. After his discharge, he returned to Jackson and practiced medicine until 1982.

Lt. Howard Lougheed, center, stands behind a sign made out of airplane parts. The Army Air Corps men designed it to mark the hospital in Watton, England.

Surgical Tech. 4 Donald H. Hartman stands next to an ambulance in Germany. Hartman served with the 85th Evacuation Hospital, 7th Army in Europe.

Tech. 5 Earl L. Hill stands next to his ambulance during an Army inspection in France. Hill was driver of ambulance No. 1 and was always the first vehicle sent out on a run.

An Army surgical team takes a break from operating. Tech. 4 Donald H. Hartman, second from left standing, assisted the medical officer during surgery, maintained sterile equipment and administered medications.

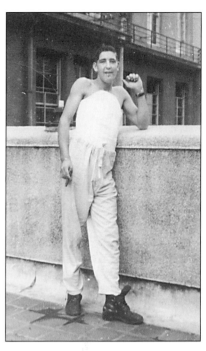

Pfc. Harrison Leverett recovers from a broken back in 1946 at the 13th Army General Hospital in Osaka, Japan.

Pfc. Allen R. Smith gets some fresh air outside the Army hospital in Naples, Italy. Smith's recovery from hepatitis took more than two months, but he later rejoined the 85th Division.

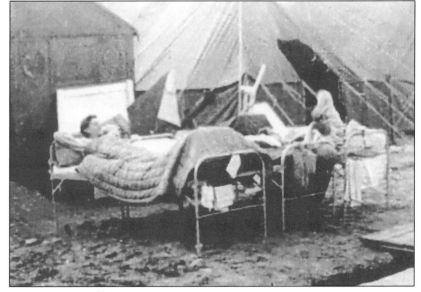

Spring in North Africa is usually rainy and cold. Army Pvt. William Hampton enjoys a rare, sunny day, thanks to the hospital wardsmen, who carted him along the muddy boardwalks to get a bit of fresh air.

Serving stateside

Pfc. Arnold Garred, right, joins fellow Army Air Corpsmen in 1944 at Lincoln Air Force Base, Neb.

Pfc. Wayne Weber checks out a big Army rig at the Diamond Reo Proving Grounds in Aberdeen, Md.

An Army Air Corps crew lines up at Pratt Army Airbase in the spring 1945. Lt. Joseph F. McCarthy, front row, fifth from right, served with the 346th Bombardment Group.

THOSE WHO SERVED

Clinton Abrams
Marines

Russell W. Anderson
Marines

Benny Augustine
Army

Frank Augustine
Army

John Augustine
Navy

Stanley Augustine
Army

Pvt. Thomas Green's official boot camp picture shows the Marines of Platoon 184 after their 1944 basic training in San Diego, Calif.

One of Pvt. Thomas Green's possessions was a handwritten copy of the Marine Rifle Creed.

My Rifle: The Creed of a US Marine

This is my rifle. There are many like it, but this one is mine.

My rifle is my best friend. It is my life. I must master it as I must master my life.

My rifle, without me, is useless. Without my rifle, I am useless. I must fire my rifle true. I must shoot straighter than my enemy who is trying to kill me. I must shoot him before he shoots me. I will...

My rifle and myself know that what counts in this war is not the rounds we fire, the noise of our burst, nor the smoke we make. We know that it is the hits that count. We will hit...

My rifle is human, even as I, because it is my life. Thus, I will learn it as a brother. I will learn its weaknesses, its strength, its parts, its accessories, its sights and its barrel. I will ever guard it against the ravages of weather and damage as I will ever guard my legs, my arms, my eyes and my heart against damage. I will keep my rifle clean and ready. We will become part of each other. We will...

Before God, I swear this creed. My rifle and myself are the defenders of my country. We are the masters of our enemy. We are the saviors of my life.

So be it, until victory is America's and there is no enemy, but peace!

Staff Sgt. Hobart "Dale" Blaisdell and Cpl. Joe Cimock find the beach of La Jolla, Calif., a bright spot to visit. Both Marines were stationed at San Diego in 1943.

THOSE WHO SERVED

Fred A. Bahlau
Army

Harold Bean
Army Air Force

Joe Bedore
Navy

David M. Bennett
Army

Gordon N. Bennett
Army Air Corps

Rex B. Bennett
Army

Merchant Marines gather on deck for a church service. Army Tech. 5 Elliott C. Amley was aboard in April 1947.

The crew of the B-17 Flying Fortress "Fighting Pappy" share a happy moment stateside July 18, 1943. The crew was later shot down on its fifth mission on Oct. 10, 1943, over Kiel, Germany. They are, back row, left to right: Staff Sgt. Walter D. Johnson, aerial gunner, ball turret; Sgt. David C. Sharman, aerial gunner, left waist; T/Sgt. Joseph Lemischak, engineer, aerial gunner, top turret; Staff Sgt. Howard D. Hinman, aerial gunner, right waist; T/Sgt. Johnie R. Bryant, radio gunner, aerial gunner; and Staff Sgt. Quentin E. Freed, aerial gunner, tail gun. Officers in front are: 2nd Lt. Vernon R. Smith, pilot; 2nd Lt. George A. Dickerson of Jackson, bombardier; 2nd Lt. Calvin F. Ford, navigator; and 2nd Lt. Robert Greenhalgh, co-pilot. Bryant was killed in action and the others became prisoners-of-war.

Those Who Served

Warren N. Bennett
Navy

Sherman W. Berkeypile
Army

Hobart Blaisdell
Marines

Kenneth A. Blanchard
Army

Madlyne Blanchard
Navy

Marion Bridenstine
Army

Machinist Mate Third Class Thomas W. Cecil gives a salute, protocol for the Navy, while boarding in September 1944 at the San Diego base.

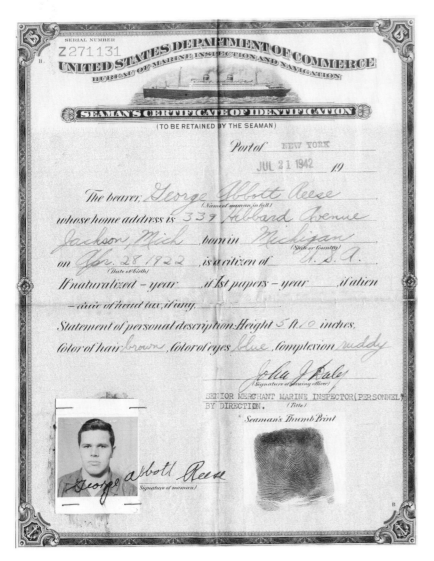

Above: Seaman First Class George Abbott Reese stops by a boat while on the shore of Hoffman Island in 1942.
Left: Reese's Merchant Marine identification papers include a personal description, photograph and thumbprint.

THOSE WHO SERVED

Herbert Brogan
Army

John W. Bryan
Army

Harold R. Buckles
Navy

Elmer Budd
Army

Robert Burdick
Army

Willard Burdick
Army

A group of Marines chide Cpl. Elwyn "Rabbit" Rider about his bald head. Rider shaved it in 1944 to fight a fungal infection while in Kaui, Hawaii.

Army Staff Sgt. Donald Field, left, checks the "Tokyo bound" message on the side of a bomb. Field would load the 300-pound bombs in the bays of B-29 and B-25 bombers near Portland, Ore.

Staff Sgt. Donald Field, front row, fourth from left, poses with his fellow Army crew members. Field worked on the Pacific coast near Portland, Ore., loading bombs on aircraft.

THOSE WHO SERVED

Louis Butcher
Navy

William E. Cadwallader
Army

W. B. "Pete" Caldwell
Army Air Force

Jack Campbell
Army

Lillian Campbell
Navy

Thomas W. Cecil
Navy

Above: Army Air Corps Flight Officer Ralph Brown and Army Sgt. Walter Clark take a rest while spending time together in Texas.
Left: Army Sgt. Clayton McNaughton, second from right, holds a flag as part of the color guard at Camp Livingston, La.

The emblem of the 119th Field Artillery was worn by a Jackson group of Army soldiers stationed in the Aleutian Islands, Alaska. The unit, originally the Coast Artillery, was a National Guard group and was one of the first to be activated at the start of the war.

The Army's 119th Field Artillery gets in some training on the Aleutian Islands, Alaska. The group originated as a former National Guard unit headquartered in Jackson.

THOSE WHO SERVED

Paul Chmielewski
Army

Margie P. Cleck
Navy

Howard Clemons
Army

Robert J. Clemons
Army

Donald Cooke
Army

Alice H. Crandall
Army

Serving in the Pacific

Marine Capt. Arthur Zenneth Pond stands next to his plane in 1942. Pond was an ace pilot who shot down at least five enemy aircraft. Pond was killed that year on Sept. 10, during the Battle of Guadalcanal. He was awarded the Navy Cross, second only to the Medal of Honor.

Cpl. Ival Hendrick checks out a piece of artillery while serving with the Army.

A series of drawings shows the movements of the Marines' 17th Anti-aircraft Artillery Battalion. Pfc. Ray "Red" Brunk was assigned to the group.

THOSE WHO SERVED

Donald V. Crandall
Army Air Corps

Paul Crandall
Navy

Wilbur Crandall
Navy

Robert C. Cross
Navy

Maryan J. Czubko
Marine Corps

Leo Davidowicz
Army

It wasn't exactly paradise under the palm trees for Petty Officer Second Class Edward R. Phelps. Phelps slept in the muggy heat of the Navy huts during his South Pacific assignments.

The team of the Navy Underwater Detection Station gathers on Samara Island in the Philippines. Petty Officer Second Class Edward R. Phelps was stationed with the group in 1943.

THOSE WHO SERVED

William M. Dennis
Army

Robert E. Deschaine
Navy

John R. DesNoyer
Army Air Force

Warren A. Dexter
Army

George A. Dickerson
Army Air Force

Russell W. Dochstader
Navy

Cpl. Lester Pond works with farmers in China, digging a slit trench. Pond was with the Army's 14th Air Force, 35th Photo Reconnaissance.

Dr. J.H. Ahronheim took an Army commission and studied the effects of combat. Capt. Ahronheim's laboratory work in the South Pacific during 1944 was in a tent with a foxhole nearby. He frequently dove into the hole during Japanese night raids.

Peeking out an air-raid shelter after a false alarm are J.B. Russell, Aviation Machinist Mate Second Class Warren Niles Bennett, and Howard Webster. The Navy men were shot down in an attack on Yap Island.

THOSE WHO SERVED

Tony Drongowski
Navy

Wilbur Dungy
Army Air Force

Joseph E. Dunigan
Army Air Force

George A. Dutton
Navy

Ed Dwojak
Marines

Leo Dwojak
Army

Staff Sgt. John M. Pieron takes a cigar break while serving in 1944 with the Army's 495th Engineer Corps in New Guinea.

Pfc. Jack Brouard, second from left, soaks up some South Pacific sun with his fellow Marines on the Russell Islands.

Workers survey construction near Milne Bay, New Guinea. Major Franklin "Jim" Tilford helped the Army build the bridge in 1943.

THOSE WHO SERVED

Lester L. Elliott
Navy

Philip Farrand
Navy

Donald Field
Army

Ethel Mae Fillhart
Navy

J. W. "Jay" Freeman
Army

David W. Fritz
Navy

The sign for the 531st Bomb Squadron of the Army's 5th Air Force features Donald Duck tossing a bomb. T/Sgt. Alden "Don" Lake flew with the group in 1944.

your son Love —

T/Sgt. Alden "Don" Lake drapes some ammunition around his neck in May 1944 before boarding an Army Air Corps bomber.

THOSE WHO SERVED

Hugh W. Fritz
Army Air Corps

Stanley F. Fryt
Army

William Fryt
Navy

Albert C. Gaige
Army

Arnold Garred
Army Air Corps

Leonard D. Gebhardt
Navy

Marine Capt. Robert Whiting stands on the wing of an F-4U-1 Corsair fighter, next to the logo of "Luscious Lil-Nan," named after his wife. Whiting was awarded the Distinguished Flying Cross as a division leader, flying 67 combat missions in which he shot down four Japanese Zeros and three probables.

Army Air Corps Crew No. 344 poses for a formal picture before heading out on a May 24, 1944, mission. They are, back row left to right: Lt. James L. Brasfield, pilot; Lt. Keith B. Cooper, co-pilot; Lt. Stephen P. Resko, navigator; and Lt. Donald E. Haven, bombardier. Front row left to right: T/Sgt. Alden "Don" Lake of Jackson, radio operator; Cpl. Albert M. Ward, engineer; Cpl. Edward M. North, assistant engineer; Cpl. Clarence L. Newton, waistgunner; Cpl. Hubert S. Boyer, gunner; and Cpl. Carl Painter, tailgunner.

THOSE WHO SERVED

William A. Gee
Coast Guard

James L. Gibson
Army

William W. Goudie
Army

Thomas Green
Marines

Gorson R. Greening
Army

Andrew Gyurkovitz
Army

Army Staff Sgt. Harold J. Tucker checks out a plane in the South Pacific. Tucker stayed in the Army for 35 more years and rose to the rank of colonel.

Marine 2nd Lt. Richard Zeller checks his plane in September 1944 on Green Island in the Solomons.

Staff Sgt. Charles E. Scott, left, stands with two of the "Flying Fiends," members of the Army Air Force's 36th Fighter Squadron, 8th Fighter Group.

THOSE WHO SERVED

Nora Hampton
Army

William J. Hampton
Army

James E. Harner
Army

Leland Harris
Navy

Don Hartman
Army

Thomas R. Hawkins
Navy

Chief Petty Officer Tony Drongowski, far right, and other sailors tackle the jungles on Isle Nou, New Caledonia, in the South Pacific.

Seaman First Class Hugh Morrow was a cook striker aboard the USS Maryland. Morrow cooked meals for more than 4,000 men, making more than 400 gallons of coffee per meal as part of Operation Magic Carpet Ride, the military's effort to repatriate troops in 1945.

Philip Farrand, Navy electrician mate first class, is ready to perform his special sea detail on the USS O'Neill — working a wench to raise the anchor.

THOSE WHO SERVED

Harold B. Hemry
Navy

Ival Hendrick
Army

Earl L. Hill
Army

Jack G. Hill
Marines

Harold H. Hively
Army Air Force

Albert Hoch
Army

Army T/Sgt. Max Ratliff poses with two native children of the Gilbert Islands. Ratliff was with the 7th Division, a medical unit that helped the wounded from the Marshall and Mariana islands. Ratliff was shipped back to Hawaii when he suffered a severe case of jaundice.

Navy Chief Petty Officer Tony Drongowski photographs his friend, Bill Stiller, overlooking the base at Isle Nou, New Caledonia. The Coral Sea site was used for ship repair in the South Pacific.

Navy Pharmacist Mate First Class Robert Wellman, left, joins brother Charles Wellman during a ship repair in Guam. Charles Wellman's rank was Navy special artificer optical second class.

Pfc. Elra Junior Wahl, second from right, lines up in April 1944 with other men from the Marines' 3rd Division, 593rd Platoon. Wahl was stationed in Guam.

THOSE WHO SERVED

Kenneth Hoch
Army

David N. Hoffman
Navy

Edward Hoffman
Navy

Herman Hoffman
Army

William Hoffman
Navy

Dale W. Hons
Army

Theodore Keyes, mailman third class, sits on the far right of the balcony of a Navy base post office near the Leyte Gulf, Philippines. Keyes was responsible for sorting top-secret mail.

Pfc. Otis Whitlock, left, looks up his cousin, Pfc. Glenn Whitlock, on June 6, 1945, at Luzon in the Philippines while both were there with the Army.

Staff Sgt. John M. Pieron drives some heavy equipment for the Army while in the Philippines.

Troops gather on a Philippine shore to get a closer look at LST-593. Army Pvt. Robert Clemons served on the ship.

THOSE WHO SERVED

Howard L. Horning
Navy

Paul E. Horning
Navy

Max Hotchkin
Army Air Corps

George R. Howard
Marines

Cyril M. Hudechek
Marines

Wendell W. Huggett
Army

Jim Richardson, Navy seaman first class, takes a picture in 1944 of the tattered palm trees and bombed-out ruins on Saipan.

The burned shell of a Japanese hangar on Saipan includes old airplane parts. Seaman First Class Jim Richardson took the photo in 1944 while serving with the Navy.

Navy Seaman First Class Jim Richardson records the destruction on Saipan in 1944. An American flag rests atop a bombed-out temple.

Those Who Served

Billy Hunt
Army

Duane Huntoon
Army

Dennis L.A. Johns
Army Air Force

Owen Johnson
Army

Forrest A. Jones
Army

Ted Jones Jr.
Army

Cpl. Leonard "Sack" W. Owczarzak stands next to a 90-mm anti-aircraft gun. The Army used the artillery to shoot down Japanese planes, close up caves and tunnels, and destroy enemy troop concentrations.

Marine Pfc. Jack Brouard hops aboard an International 6 x 6 truck. Brouard drove the vehicle while serving 26 months in the South Pacific islands during 1944 and 1945.

A row of duck boats and other amphibious vehicles are lined up behind Army Pfc. Wayne Weber in Nagasaki, Japan.

THOSE WHO SERVED

Lozell T. Jordon
Army Air Corps

Robert Kendall Jr.
Army Air Corps

Theodore Keyes
Navy

Ray H. King
Army

John Kohn
Army

Andy Kokoczka
Army

Flashy "nose art" looks over a crew of Army Air Force men in the Pacific. The bomb insignias, upper left, kept track of the number of missions, and the Japanese flags tallied the number of downed enemy planes. Nose art was forbidden later during the war, and "Thunderhead" was removed.

Standing left to right are: Capt. Ted Morgan, pilot; 1st Lt. Hervey F. Paradis, co-pilot; 1st Lt. Edward Septowski, flight engineer; 1st Lt. Eugene R. Wallworth, bombardier; and 1st Lt. Robert L. Ullman, navigator.

Kneeling left to right: Staff Sgt. William E. Furman, left gunner; T/Sgt. William E. Smith Jr., central fire control gunner; Staff Sgt. Harold J. Tucker of Jackson, right gunner; Staff Sgt. Richard D. Isles, radio operator; Staff Sgt. Kenneth W. LaMone, radio operator; and Staff Sgt. Warner C. Grindem, tailgunner.

THOSE WHO SERVED

Frank Kokoczka
Army

Joseph Kokoczka
Army

Leo Kokoczka
Army

Martin Kokoczka
Army

Alfred Konkol
Army

John Kurpinski
Army

1st Lt. J.W. "Jay" Weeks climbs into a P-47 fighter plane while serving with the Army Air Force. Weeks' assignment was with the 5th Emergency Rescue Squad doing air-sea rescues.

A view of Mount Fuji, or Fuji-yama, in Japan is captured on film by Army Cpl. Austin Ladd while flying overhead in 1945.

LST-924 loads up troops and supplies at Leyte Island in the Philippines. Army Pvt. Robert Clemons witnessed the landing.

The hot weather on Biak Island, Dutch East Indies, forces Army Air Force pilots to go shirtless. From left, they are: Lt. Col. Claude Spencer of Jackson, Harold Albertson, Garvin Morris, Claude Carpenter and Ken McIntosh.

THOSE WHO SERVED

John Kwiatkowski
Army

Walter Kwiatkowski
Army

Austin Ladd
Army

Bill L. Lairson
Army

Alden "Don" Lake
Army Air Corps

Stuart E. Lake
Army

Navy Seaman First Class Anthony Zaski (Zakrzewski), right, enjoys some camaraderie with a couple of sailors.

Navy Machinist Mate Second Class Ronald Wyatt, left, stands on deck of the LST-595 in the Philippines along with Max Rivitzer, center, and Bill Horton, right.

Seaman Second Class Robert L. Freeman, left, goes shirtless to enjoy the sunshine aboard a Navy ship in the Pacific.

Seaman First Class Ralph Robinson plays with Gizmo, the mascot of Navy ship USS LSM-34 on a central Philippine island beach. The two were enjoying a break in action around April 1945 after many landings on enemy soil. The ship's original landing came Oct. 20, 1944, on Leyte Island under General Douglas MacArthur.

THOSE WHO SERVED

Wayne Larson
Navy

Philip Leathead
Army Air Corps

Philip J. Lee
Army Air Force

Stuart R. Leigh
Marine Corps

Harrison Leverett
Army

Adam Lewandowski
Army

Sailors on Guam in 1945 include Robert "Bubs" Richardson, Navy machinist mate third class, second from left.

Sgt. Charles Maynard Otto, right, and three of his Army buddies show off the suntans they acquired in 1945 while on Guam.

Navy Machinist Mate Second Class Ronald G. Wyatt, back, barters with native children in Manila, Philippines. Wyatt gave the kids chewing gum in exchange for local money.

THOSE WHO SERVED

Robert Linden
Army

Victor Linden
Army

Cleo Harold Lorencen
Army

Howard J. Lougheed
Army Air Corps

Nick Luppo
Navy

Aleck Mandreger
Army Air Force

Rows of tents belonging to American troops cover the landscape on Okinawa. Sgt. Charles Maynard Otto was part of the Army's force in 1945.

Army men gather near an old Japanese boxcar left at a station on Okinawa. Sgt. Charles Maynard Otto, back standing, goes through the damaged area in 1945.

A sign from the 316th Bomb Wing Division lists the groups who fought at Okinawa. Army Cpl. Austin Ladd snapped a photo in 1945 of the sign.

Sgt. Charles Maynard Otto, front right, gets a look at an old Japanese railroad car. Otto was with the Army near Naha, Okinawa, in 1945.

THOSE WHO SERVED

Eugene Markiewicz
Army

Leonard Markiewicz
Army

Albert T. Maybourne
Navy

George W. McAtee
Army

James K. McConnell
Army

William H. McDermott
Army

Army Cpl. Austin Ladd, far left, befriends some of the residents on Okinawa in 1945.

Pfc. Glenn Whitlock, back row right, checks out a Japanese flag, featuring the Rising Sun. Whitlock and his Army buddies were camped in a rest area near Pugo, Japan.

Army Cpl. Austin Ladd's photo of "Snipers' Hill" on Okinawa shows the difficult terrain that had to be taken during the battles of 1945.

THOSE WHO SERVED

Thomas McInerney
Army Air Force

Clayton McNaughton
Army

Arthur L. Middlebrook
Army

Clayton Miller
Army

Rolf Moeckel
Army

Ralph Montgomery
Army

Above: LSM-43 makes its way through the water to land on Iwo Jima. Sgt. Maryan Czubko was part of the Marine invasion.
Right: Czubko's tank bulldozes a front-line path during the battle of Iwo Jima. Two days later, the tank was destroyed when it hit a land mine.

The USS Loeser cuts through the South Pacific on its way to do battle at Luzon, Philippines and Iwo Jima. Serving on board was Navy Machinist Mate Second Class Paul E. Horning.

THOSE WHO SERVED

Richard L. Morris
Army

Dr. Nathan Munro
Navy

Herbert Nash

Louis O'Connell
Army

James O'Leary
Navy

Leonard Owczarzak
Army

Lt. William Rumler, front row, left, gets together with fellow Army Air Corps pilots one last time just before discharge. They are members of the China, Burma, India group and belong to the Hump Pilots Association.

Above: Radioman Second Class Paul Crandall, right, walks the streets in China with some other Navy sailors. Left: Seaman Second Class John L. Vincent Jr. finds a relaxing spot aboard the cruiser USS Nashville in September 1945 while docked at Shanghai, China.

THOSE WHO SERVED

Leo Pec
Army

Wendell W. Phillips
Army

John Pieron
Army

Leo Piotrowski
Army

John Piper
Army

Richard Piper
Navy

A junkyard of planes is stockpiled near Ryukyus, near the west coast of Okinawa. Army Air Force Sgt. Robert Wellman took the photograph.

Army Air Corps Sgt. Robert Wellman checks out a tank on the beach of Ie Shima. Ie Shima is part of Okinawa and the island where journalist Ernie Pyle was killed.

Army Sgt. Charles Maynard Otto checks out an abandoned outpost after the 1945 Battle of Okinawa. Otto noted "tomb" on the photo, signifying the possibility of dead Japanese soldiers. Otto served as a construction foreman with Company A of the 1885th Army Engineers.

THOSE WHO SERVED

Arthur Z. Pond
Marine Corps

Lester Pond
Army Air Force

Keith Porlier
Navy

Donald Powell
Army

Vincent Raciboski
Army

Max Ratliff
Army

Electrician Mate Third Class Norman Ulrich, center, grabs a few moments of downtime with his fellow Navy shipmates aboard the USS LST-1063.

Army Pfc. Glenn Whitlock takes a break from his bicycle ride outside a ball-bearing factory near Takatsuki, Japan. Whitlock was stationed there with the Army in the fall of 1945.

Above: Seaman First Class Charles Walker, left, celebrates the Japanese surrender with Navy shipmates. The sailors were in Yokohama, Japan, during September 1945.
Left: Japanese prisoners congregate on the deck of LCI-644. The group had surrendered on the Okinawa beach toward the end of the war. Carl Heath, Seaman second class, looks over the captives.

THOSE WHO SERVED

Edward Reeve
Army

Donald Reynolds
Army

Edwin C. Reynolds
Army

Robert Reynolds
Navy

Burton Richardson
Army

Gale D. Richardson
Navy

Marine Cpl. Elwyn "Rabbit" Rider photographs Japanese civilians going through a military garbage truck near Saga, Japan. Food was scarce after the atomic attack of Hiroshima, so the servicemen deliberately left edible items on the truck for the scavengers.

Navy Seaman First Class Carl Heath takes a picture of a shipyard in Yokosuka, Japan, after the surrender. The boats were abandoned and never completed.

The ruins of Tachikawa, Japan, are photographed Nov. 1, 1945, by Army Air Corps 1st Lt. Philip Leathead. The town, located outside Tokyo, was bombed by American forces. Leathead was a B-24 pilot assigned to the 494th Bombardment Group, nicknamed "Kelley's Kobras," the last bomb group formed during the war.

THOSE WHO SERVED

James M. Richardson
Navy

George Robins
Army

Willard B. Ruede
Army Air Force

Ken Salsbury
Army Air Corps

Phyllis J. Salsbury
Navy

Leonard J. Schweda
Navy

Lt. General Timoshiro Kawabe is en route to sign the Japanese peace treaty. Army Air Force Sgt. Major Joseph Dunigan photographed the delegate on the way to the historic meeting.

Above: Tech. 5 Elliott C. Amley was in Kobe, Japan, in 1947 as part of the U.S. Army's occupational forces. Left: The Japanese surrender delegation arrives on Ie Shima on Aug. 19, 1945. The group transferred to an American C-54 transport plane destined for negotiations in Manilla. Army Air Force Sgt. Robert Wellman photographed the event.

THOSE WHO SERVED

Charles E. Scott
Army Air Corps

Maynard Scott
Navy

Virginia I. Scott
Navy

Donald E. Shewman
Navy

Joseph Sierminski Jr.
Army

Andrew Skrzynski
Army

USS LST-1063 beaches on the shore of Okinawa shortly after the war's end. Norman Ulrich, Navy electrician mate third class, served on the ship in 1945-46.

Seaman First Class Carl Heath, left, talks with two other sailors about the end of the war while aboard LCI-644.

"Betty bombers" land on Ie Shima bringing Japanese officials. Gen. Douglas MacArthur ordered the planes to be painted white with a green cross on the tail, replacing the Rising Sun symbol. Army Air Force Sgt. Robert Wellman recorded the historic landing.

THOSE WHO SERVED

Mitchell F. Skrzynski
Army

Edward C. Slugay
Navy

Allen R. Smith
Army

Donald B. Smith
Army

Fred J. Smith
Army

John E. Smith
Army

Marine Pfc. Ray "Red" Brunk checks out a piece of abandoned artillery left in a Japanese pillbox on Tinian Island.

Pfc. Harrison Leverett, left, relaxes outside an Army shack in Osaka, Japan, in 1946.

Army Tech. 5 Elliott C. Amley Jr. supervises a happy work group in Kobe, Japan. In 1947, Amley was in charge of a beer warehouse.

1st Lt. Philip Leathead, center, joins some of his Army Air Corps friends in Tachikawa, Japan. Navigator Lloyd Stott, left, and Bombardier Richard MacDonald visit Leathead during a three-month stint after the war.

THOSE WHO SERVED

Rolland M. Smith
Army Air Corps

Claude Spencer
Army Air Force

Clarence St. John
Army

Larry Strickrodt
Army

Thomas M. Sussex
Army

Lucille Sweet
Navy

Serving in Europe

Little dog "Winnie," serves as the mascot of the Army Air Corps crew of "Patches," a B-17 that was later shot down on Oct. 14, 1942, while on a mission to Schweinfurt, Germany.
The crew are back row, left to right: 2nd Lt. Robert B. Kilmer, 1st Lt. William H. Wilson, 1st Lt. John Barkley and 1st Lt. Donald P. Oglivie.
Front row, left to right: Staff Sgt. Francis R. Sylvia, T/Sgt. James Murray, Staff Sgt. William E. Martin, Staff Sgt. James W. McKeon, T/Sgt. Emmett A. Hood and Staff Sgt. Louis L. Ratkiewicz of Jackson, the tailgunner.

THOSE WHO SERVED

James H. Swihart
Navy

Elmer Syrjamaki
Army

Paul Taylor
Navy

Jim Tilford
Army

Steve Trujillo
Army

Harold Tucker
Army Air Force

Above: Some friends join Army Air Force Master Sgt. John DesNoyer, right on cannon, atop Edinburgh Castle in England.
Left: DesNoyer stops in front of the barracks that housed the 8th Air Force in England.

Tech. 5 Lyle Walworth drives his fellow soldiers around Belfast, Ireland, in 1943. Walworth was a member of the Army's 1st Armored Division, 11th Armored Infantry.

1st. Lt. James Edward White covers some ground around Berlin on his motorcycle. White flew with the 9th Air Force, 406 Fighter Group.

THOSE WHO SERVED

Harry F. Twardowski
Army

Joseph Twardowski
Army

Theresa Twardowski
Navy

Norman Ulrich
Navy

Charles VanAkin
Army

Steve Vaurek
Army

1st Sgt. James Kenneth McConnell takes his German motorcycle for a ride in 1943 while stationed in Europe with the Army.

Pfc. Andrew Gyurkovitz takes in some of the sights and architecture of Italy in 1942. Gyurkovitz worked as an Army automotive mechanic.

Pfc. Stuart E. Lake, left, is photographed with fellow soldiers in 1943. Lake was part of Army special forces in Africa, Belgium, France and Germany.

Brothers Sgt. Joseph Lacinski, left, and Tech. 3 Bernard Lacinski rendezvous in Prezenzano, Italy, in the spring of 1943. They both served in the Army and met up during a softening of the artillery.

THOSE WHO SERVED

Stanley Vavryca
Army

Thomas Vincent
Navy

Fred Vinton
Marines

Arnold Waltz
Merchant Marines

Lyle Walworth
Army

John L. Weatherwax
Army Air Corps

Cpl. T/5 J.W. "Jay" Freeman and other members of an Army motor pool try to keep warm before the Battle of the Bulge. Temperatures in France dropped to 20 below zero. "Oui-oui" the dog was the group's mascot, a gift from a local Frenchman.

1st Sgt. Steve Trujillo, left, takes a break from the action in France 1944 with a few Army buddies.

Army Cpl. Gerald Porter, center, looks messy after making his way through France. Porter writes, "You can see who does all the fighting in this war, the one with the two guns."

A cup of coffee and a doughnut warm Army soldiers in Nancy, France. The Red Cross clubmobile fed the men in 1944, including Sgt. T/5 Albert Gaige.

THOSE WHO SERVED

Claire Weber
Navy

John Weber Jr.
Navy

Wayne Weber
Army

Frank Wellman
Navy

Robert E. Wellman
Army Air Force

James E. White
Army Air Force

Sgt. T/5 Albert Gaige takes aim at a target while in France.

Donald Brininstool, left, poses with other members of the Army's 101st Airborne Division, 506th Parachute Infantry Regiment. Brininstool parachuted with the group into Normandy on D-Day, June 6, 1944, and also fought in the Battle of the Bulge at Bastogne, Belgium.

Lt. Howard H. Robb, an Army Air Corps pilot, stands next to a B-24 bomber nicknamed "Fearless Fosdick," a comic-strip character in "Li'l Abner."

THOSE WHO SERVED

Glenn Whitlock
Army

Clark Winchell
Army

Robert Woodworth
Navy

Ronald Wyatt
Navy

Chester D. Young
Marines

John J. Zaborowski
Army

The B-24 Army Air Force crew, 2nd bomb Division, 14th Combat Wing, 44th Bomb Group, 67th Bomb Squadron, discusses its completed D-Day mission — destroying a crossroad at St. Laurent sur Mer, France. They are front row, left to right: an unknown intelligence officer; Pilot Robert P. Knowles; Navigator John E. Butler; Engineer Francis T. Ryan; Radio Operator Michael A. Powers; Waistgunner Henry E. Lavallee; Bombardier John A. Fenn; and Co-pilot Lt. Howard H. Robb of Jackson.
Back row: Tailgunner William S. Guess and Nosegunner Russell B. Lindsey.

Staff Sgt. Fred Bahlau storms the Normandy beach on D-Day plus 4. Bahlau earned two silver and two bronze stars during the invasion as a paratrooper in the Army's 101st Airborne Division.

Allied troops in Weymouth, England, line up to board the ships for the D-Day invasion. The picture was taken June 4, 1944, by Leonard Gebhardt, a coxswain on a Navy amphibious landing vehicle. Gebhardt's ship made 45 trips before sinking off the beach at Normandy.

THOSE WHO SERVED

Julius Zakrzewski
Army

Richard Zakrzewski
Navy

Richard Zeller
Marine Corps

Harold Ziegler
Army

William R. Zimmer
Army

Master Sgt. John DesNoyer stands at the doorway of the 8th Air Force's office in England in 1944.

Army paratrooper Clarence St. John and Navy coxswain Leonard Gebhardt exchange hometown talk while meeting in 1944 in England.

LST-312 suffers major damage after being hit by a buzz-bomb near London. The July 6, 1944, explosion killed six enlisted men and two officers.

Lt. Robert T. Kendall Jr.'s plane burns at Poddington, England, on Aug. 4, 1944. Kendall, an Army Air Corps bombardier, was on his fourth mission with the B-17 when it was hit by fire from a German fighter. The bomber flew back in flames and was completely consumed minutes after the crew deboarded. Kendall served in 27 missions with the 12th Bomber Group of the 325th Squadron.

Pvt. John Piper was the first Jackson-area Army soldier reported missing in action in North Africa. Piper spent two years and three months as a German prisoner-of-war in Stalag 3-B. He was captured Feb. 17, 1943, in Tunisia.

Cpl. Everett C. Farr, back row left, stops for a break in 1944 on the steps of an Army Air Corps Quonset hut in Norwich, England.

Army Tech. 5 Lyle Walworth watches over a group of German prisoners-of-war while stationed in 1944 in Italy.

Staff Sgt. Guy Robert Champney gets ready to leave on a B-24 mission in Fogia, Italy. Champney was an engineer/topgunner with the Army Air Corps.

Pfc. Allen R. Smith, left, grabs a Jeep ride from a fellow soldier in Italy. Smith served as radioman moving communication systems for the 85th Army Division.

Staff Sgt. Kenneth Broughton, back row, second from right, flew 50 missions with his B-17 crew. The bomb group tallied 25 missions over Italy with the 15th Army Air Force, and was shipped to England to do 25 more with the 8th Air Force. All came home safely.

Army Cpl. T/5 J.W. "Jay" Freeman, right, stands underneath two teetering train cars after a 1944 bombing of Bonn, Germany.

Army Pfc. John Winchell stops at a German house in 1944.

Sgt. Robert W. Stoddard and Sgt. Richard C. Stoddard pose next to "Skipper," an Army Air Corps B-24 Liberator, at Spinnazola Airbase, Italy. At their mother's request, a special exemption was granted allowing the twins to fly more than 50 missions together. After a furlough home, the pair returned to duty aboard a troop train that collided Sept. 14, 1944, near Terre Haute, Ind. Robert Stoddard was killed, and Richard Stoddard was hospitalized for a year.

Pfc. Chuck Hudson enjoys a sunny morning after spending a snowy night in his tent during the Battle of the Bulge. Hudson was with the Army's 31st Anti-aircraft Artillery, 113th AAA Gun Battalion.

The "Big B Bridge" near Berlin designates mileage to some American cities. Army Tech. 5 William R. Zimmer surveys the route shortly after the 1944 Battle of the Bulge.

Tech. 5 William R. Zimmer sits on a bomb dud in Bonn, Germany. Zimmer was assigned in 1944 to the Army's 113th Anti-aircraft Battalion.

"Fighters Up," a book authored by Eric Friedheim and Samuel W. Taylor, features a story about T/Sgt. Dennis L.A. Johns. Johns was shot down and was a German prisoner-of-war for two years.
The 1945 book was one of the first published after the war, retelling the feats of the 8th and 9th Army Air Forces.

Oil smoke and flak blur the skies during a 1944 Army Air Force bombing over Vienna. Staff Sgt. Philip J. Lee was aboard the B-24 during its mission.

Army Sgt. Donald Brininstool, center, smiles along with his fellow paratroopers in Austria on V-E Day, May 8, 1945.

Pfc. Stanley Augustine, front row right, lines up in Germany with his Army squad in front of a howitzer cannon.

Cpl. Gerald Porter peeks from his foxhole during a break in action while serving with the Army in Germany.

Army T/5 Sgt. Harold Lorencen gases up a military truck while serving with Company F of the 271st Infantry in Europe.

Army Sgt. John C. Parylak and Cpl. Edward "Ted" Reeve of the 207th Field Artillery Battalion fire a German anti-tank gun against the enemy. The pair retrieved the abandoned gun during a battle lull in January 1945. They snuck across the Roer River in Holland and brought back the cannon and shells. Parylak, left gunnery, loses his helmet during the explosion. Reeve, right, working as forward observer, covers his ears, but still suffered permanent hearing loss.
In the air above, liaison pilot 2nd Lt. John Dianich relays the battle movements to the ground troops.

Tech. 5 Dale Hons, left, stands with fellow Army engineers, Daniel Marthe and Garland Kinsey, in front of "Ann," the truck named after Kinsey's girlfriend.

Pfc. Edward Donald Hammond named his Army Jeep "the Wolverine," after his home state. Hammond inspects the vehicle June 18, 1945, in Whitlich, Germany.

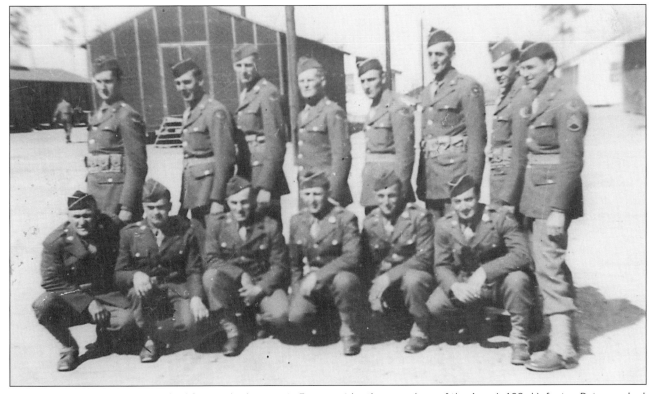

Sgt. Richard D. Bater, back row, third from right, lines up in Europe with other members of the Army's 103rd Infantry. Bater worked with landmines, working along the Rhine River.

Pfc. Sherman Berkeypile Sr., right front, stands at the head of his tank. Berkeypile drove the vehicle in 1945 while serving in Germany with the Army's Company B, 661st Tank Destroyer Battalion.

Above: Army Sgt. Jack Campbell and Cpl. Hugh Lee enjoy some spoils of war — wine from Adolf Hitler's mountain retreat in Berchtesgaden, Germany.
Right: Army Sgt. T/5 Albert Gaige finds the bombed-out ruins of Adolf Hitler's mountain retreat May 7, 1945, at Berchtesgaden, Germany, near the Austrian border. In 1938, British Prime Minister Neville Chamberlain met Hitler at the site, resulting in the Munich Agreement.

Army Cpl. Gerald Porter, right, displays a Nazi flag confiscated during a shakedown July 22, 1945, in Grunberg, Germany. Porter stayed on the second floor of the "Uberschule," the former high school in the background.

Above: Tech. 4 Donald H. Hartman sits on his bed while stationed at Ellswangen, Germany. The cot was not Army issue but one he had taken from a former German school.
Left: Tech. 5 Dale W. Hons helped build 13 bridges in Europe as a member of the Army Engineers. While in Warburg, Germany, Hons enjoys his favorite truck, dubbed "Ann" by its previous driver.

Army Pfc. John Winchell relaxes against a cigarette machine while stationed in Germany.

Above: "Kilroy was here" was a widely circulated graffiti marking drawn during World War II. It represented the U.S. super-GI who had already been at the location before the others arrived. It became a challenge to write the logo in unlikely places. The original wording was lifted from the inside of troop ships, mimicking an inspection mark left by James Kilroy, a shipyard worker in Quincy, Mass. The historic symbol is engraved on the World War II memorial in Washington, D.C.

Right: Army Tech. 5 Bill Goudie gets a picture of a German town with its buildings still draped with Nazi flags. The picture was taken before the arrival of American troops.

Allied bombings destroyed the buildings of Kassel, Germany. The ruins were photographed by Army Sgt. T/5 Albert Gaige in 1945.

Some Army soldiers grab a Nazi flag in May 1945. Tech. 5 Ralph Montgomery, front right seated, enjoys the souvenir shot.

Army Cpl. T/5 J.W. "Jay" Freeman sits on the wing of a downed Nazi plane in the German forest.

An anti-tank gun mounted on the rear of an Army truck, foreground, makes its way along a mountain trail outside of Nuremberg, Germany. Sgt. T/5 Albert Gaige records the April 1945 movement. The enemy vehicles along the roadside had been taken just a half hour earlier.

Tech. 5 Earl L. Hill checks out the ravaged remains of a concentration camp near Ingolstadt, Germany. Hill was an Army ambulance driver in May 1945 who transported the sick from hospitals and prison camps during the evacuation effort.

An American tank is put out of commission and abandoned on the outskirts of Nuremberg, Germany. Army Sgt. T/5 Albert Gaige captured the image.

Army Sgt. T/5 Albert Gaige photographs a tank shoving a truck off the road outside Nuremberg, Germany.

A derailed locomotive lays on its side in Nuremberg, Germany. Army Sgt. T/5 Albert Gaige was one of the onlookers.

Army paratrooper Staff Sgt. Fred Bahlau, left, sits in Hermann Goering's car that was left in Austria. Goering was Reich marshal and second in command behind Adolf Hitler.

Above: Enjoying the company of Elizabeth Molnar of Hungary is Army Sgt. T/5 Albert Gaige. The couple met in Salzburg, Austria. Right: Army Sgt. Jack Campbell takes a picture of a former German prison camp near Austria after its liberation in 1945.

Above: Sgt. Joseph A. Weiler gets close to an abandoned enemy tank left up in the British zone in Germany. Weiler served as an Army heavy weapons infantry leader.
Left: Herbert Louis Nash, right, rides on the back of a gendarmerie's motorcycle. Nash was a criminal investigative agent who lived in civilian homes. While in France, he investigated all types of crimes, including murders, sexual attacks, misuse of authority and black marketing. He was a witness at 20 court martials.

Staff Sgt. Louis L. Ratkiewicz, sitting right with child on lap, enjoys a moment of safety with other Army Air Corps men near Verdun, France, some time after Oct. 14, 1943. The crew's plane had been shot down and they were being hidden by the French Underground. The men walked out of France to Switzerland and then on to Italy and American lines.

Army Staff Sgt. Larry Strickrodt helps a family in the French countryside bring in their crops. The family shared the event by taking a photo and sending a copy home to Strickrodt's family.

A group of Army soldiers visits a liberated Paris in 1945 and makes a stop at the Arc de Triumph. Sgt. T/5 Marion Bridenstine, fifth from left, shares the happy occasion.

Army Sgt. Elmer Syrjamaki photographs the street sellers in Reims, France. They sold Normandy lace after the war's end.

Some of the men from the Army's 310th Field Artillery, 79th Division, celebrate victory Aug. 1, 1945, at the Arc de Triumph in Paris. T/Sgt. Norman Slusser, front row, eighth from left, enjoyed the event.

Paris was a happy city after its liberation from the Germans in 1945. Master Sgt. Lozell T. Jordon, center, poses with some of his Army Air Corps friends in front of the Arc de Triumph.

Lt. Harold Hively, pilot of a B-25 Mitchell bomber with the 12th Air Force, helped destroy the French battleship Strasbourg in Toulon harbor. To the left, keeled over, is a cruiser that was also shelled by Allied Forces.

Army Staff Sgt. Fred Bahlau, front with camera, enjoys the scenery in the Alps in 1946. Bahlau retrieved the camera from the body of a German soldier earlier in the war.

Servicemen and officers wait for instructions before shipping out for home. Lt. J.W. "Jay" Weeks was among the soldiers leaving Europe from the Army airbase at Colchester, England.

Tech. 5 Elliott C. Amley checks out an Army recruiting poster in Naples, Italy. The sign encourages the enlisted men to stay in the service after the war.

Tech. 5 Jack Eugene Weible marries Edeltraud Ruthild Domin, a German refugee whose family was displaced during the war. The couple met while Weible was part of occupational forces of Headquarters Troop, 22nd Constabulary Squadron.

Army Sgt. Elmer Syrjamaki, second right, chats with his buddies at a restaurant in Amsterdam. The group met in January 1946.

Rest and recreation

Pfc. Chester W. Leffler enjoys some reading material during his 1944 Army Air Corps stint in Stillwater, Okla.

Seaman First Class Nick Luppo, right, gets his last bit of recreation before shipping out. Luppo served in the Navy as a gunner on a Liberty ship.

Marine Sgt. Maryan J. Czubko, seated middle, makes his way through his "first and last martini." Czubko was fulfilling a promise to a fellow soldier. The Marines were celebrating their return in 1945 after occupation duty in Nagasaki, Japan.

Above: T/Sgt. W.B. "Pete" Caldwell of the Army Air Force and friend Bill Fisher chat during an evening at Kline's restaurant in San Antonio, Texas. They were discussing the end of the war.

Right: Seaman First Class Jim Richardson chums it up with his Navy buddies June 30, 1944, at the beach in Oceanside, Calif. Richardson, second from right, called the group "A bunch of Salty Boys from the Amphibious Pacific Fleet."

Navy Seaman First Class Howard L. Horning and brother Paul E. Horning, machinist mate second class, show some brotherly love after reuniting while on leave in Hawaii.

The USO canteen at Camp Kamuela, Kauai, in Hawaii gave Marine Cpl. Elwyn "Rabbit" Rider a place to enjoy a wild pig roast with his 5th Division platoon buddies.

Navy Electrician Mate Third Class Norman Ulrich, second from right, joins his Navy shipmates from LST-1063 for some refreshments. The group took a break in 1945 in Hawaii.

Army Air Force Sgt. Maj. Joseph E. Dunigan holds one of his buddies atop his shoulders in a W. Palm Beach, Fla., pool. Dunigan was cooling off in October 1943.

Army Tech. 5 Jack E. Weible takes a look around after a swimming workout in Germany. After the war ended, Weible stayed with the Headquarters troop, 22nd Constabulary Squadron, as part of the occupational forces.

Pfc. Ray "Red" Brunk, left, and two of his Marine buddies use a makeshift basketball hoop in November 1944 while stationed on Tinian.

Army Cpl. Herbert T. Brogan, front row, second from left, played some basketball on the Camp Edwards team after returning from overseas. Camp Edwards is located in Falmouth, Mass., and housed more than 2,000 German prisoners-of-war.

Capt. Rolland M. Smith, third from left, joins some of his Army Air Corps buddies for a game of basketball while stationed in China.

Servicemen spend an evening of relaxation at a USO dance in Belleville, Ill. Army Air Force Sgt. Robert Wellman, back right, enjoys the sound of the orchestra.

Above: Jack Benny, left, grabs the hand of Carol Landis during a USO show in the South Pacific. Army Cpl. Harold Mink took the picture. Right: Comedian Joe E. Brown entertains in July 1943 in Hawaii. Pfc. Glenn Whitlock snapped the picture while sitting in the audience with his Army buddies.

Recovering patients get some cheer from starlet Frances Langford and comedy legend Bob Hope. The pair entertains the sick in the spring of 1944 at the 81st Station Hospital in Bizerte, North Africa. Army Cpl. William J. Hampton captured the performance.

Clark Gable pays a visit April 5, 1943, to the 8th Air Force in Lancaster, England. Sgt. John DesNoyer grabbed a peek at the Hollywood star.

Letters to home

Shirley Burdick, mother of Willard and Bob, checks Grandma Stewart's mailbox in Leslie for any war correspondence.

While other Army soldiers relax on each side of him, Staff Sgt. Larry Strickrodt writes home from England in 1943.

A Christmas card of the USS Chester from Jim Richardson, seaman first class, wishes his parents "a very merry Christmas," and touts them as "The best Mother and Father in the world." The Navy man spent the 1944 holiday aboard ship.

Pfc. Ray "Red" Brunk sends a Christmas greeting on a postcard from the Mariana Islands. Brunk spent the 1944 holiday on Tinian with the Marines.

Army Cpl. T/5 J.W. "Jay" Freeman sends his wife, Billye, a satirical postcard May 19, 1943, featuring Adolf Hitler on a toilet as "The Bowl Gazer." Freeman pens a note claiming "Here's the picture of the man I am going after. He will be in the same place he is in this picture, when this is over with ..."

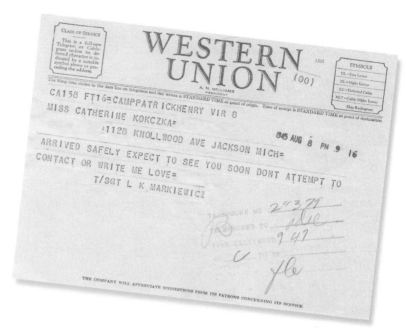

Above: T/Sgt. Leonard Markiewicz sends a telegram Aug. 8, 1945, to his fiancé, Catherine Kokoczka (Kokczka). Markiewicz had not been home from the Army in more than four and a half years. During August 1944, he was hospitalized in London for a battle wound and could not make it home for his mother's funeral.
Left: Markiewicz snuggles close to girlfriend Catherine Kokoczka while home on Army leave Dec. 28, 1941. The pair had met earlier while working at the Regent Cafe. Markiewicz suffered a groin wound fighting in Luxembourg and was one of the first servicemen to be treated with experimental penicillin.

Above: Mail carrier John Bryant delivers to 314 N. Pleasant St., home of servicemen Robert "Bob" and Willard Burdick.
Left: Pfc. Clark Winchell takes a break to write a letter home. Winchell was fighting with the Army in 1945 near Hammelburg, Germany.

On the homefront

Goodyear Tire & Rubber employees show off garden utensils used in Victory gardens. Left to right are Doris English, Richard Young, William Davis and Margaret Konkol. The company offered plots to any employee who would work them.

Wilferd T. Layton, 719 Ellery St., receives a measured amount of gasoline during 1944-45 for his 1935 Chevrolet. Gas rationing was monitored and policed for black marketing.

Rationing creates a long line at George Barrett's Service Station, 912-196 E. Ganson St. The item in demand is beer. Customers line up for their daily allotment of six bottles.

There are wars, and then there is the war that shaped our lives as we know them.

Whether you are 9 or 90, World War II created the society you live in.

Before 1941, there was no DDT, radar, jet engines, sulfa drugs, rayon, napalm, bazookas, income-tax withholding, ball-point pens, or many of the other things we take for granted today.

It was a war that touched every life. Some 8,000 Jackson residents served in the armed forces. The Citizen Patriot reported 269 were killed. Uncounted hundreds were wounded, some losing arms, legs and soundness of mind.

Thousands of Jacksonians served voluntarily as air-raid and fire wardens, first-aid and nutrition workers, hospital orderlies and cooks.

Many lost their jobs in auto plants and went to work in defense plants. Farmers moved by the millions into the cities to work. City folks flocked to the country to cultivate their "victory gardens."

Schoolchildren toted dimes to school and tin cans to movie theaters. The dimes bought Savings Stamps, which were pasted into booklets to buy War Bonds. The tin cans bought a free ticket to the movie.

On one Saturday in June 1943, some 2,300 children turned in 20 cans each to see a Gene Autry movie at Jackson's Capitol Theater. The kids "were content to sit two in a seat," according to theater officials. More than four tons of cans were collected.

In the course of the war, more than

15 million Americans moved to new homes in the greatest migration in the nation's history — greater even than the settling of the West.

In two years, California gained 1.4 million residents. The South actually lost a million residents, but its major industrial centers gained population.

The War Production Board ordered an end to all manufacturing of non-defense goods requiring the use of iron or steel. More than 400 items, ranging from bathtubs to waste baskets and including Christmas decorations, were banned from production.

All civilian auto production was stopped, putting the brakes on an industry that produced four times more cars than the rest of the world combined.

Also halted was the sale of new cars and trucks, leaving dealers with 650,000 vehicles on hand, 350 in Jackson. Prices were frozen and sales, allowed only for lend-lease, government or "essential civilian" purposes, didn't require the services of salesmen. They joined the ranks of the unemployed or went to work in the defense factories.

Sugar purchases were limited to 12 ounces per person a week. Gasoline was rationed, with citizens lining up to buy annual "car tags" for $5. The penalty for driving without the federal tag was a $25 fine and 30 days in jail.

There were things even more frightening than sugar and gasoline rationing.

The Office of Price Administration announced that the rubber shortage would put a strain on the supply ➡

The billboard of the Regent Theatre, 201-205 Francis St., showcases "Hitler — Beast of Berlin." The 1939 black-and-white film was originally banned as too inflammatory, but after some cutting it was re-released. The 87-minute movie features Alan Ladd in a supporting role and was retitled "Hell's Devils" in the early 1940s. Its first showing in Jackson was June 1943.

of girdles. The nation was expected to run out in 1943. Golf balls, sink stoppers and other rubber products faced a similar fate.

William Sparks, Jackson industrialist and builder of the Cascades, donated his 46-foot, Florida-based cruiser, the "Mathilda J," to the Navy. The boat, with its two 200-horsepower engines, was well-known as the fastest of its kind in Miami Bay.

Arthur D. Knapp, president and general manager of Mechanical Products Inc., turned over his airplane, a Lockheed "Orion," for use in hunting submarines in coastal waters and for aerial photography.

Men began wearing "Victory Suits," without vests, cuffs, pleats, belts or suspenders. The new fashion would save three-quarters of a yard of wool per suit and 30 million yards annually, according to the government.

Women's nightgowns were limited to a length of 54 inches for size 36 and "corresponding limits for other sizes." Also banned were "frills on nighties, slips, petticoats and pajamas."

Motorists were asked to drive no faster than 40 miles an hour to save gasoline and rubber. Jackson County Sheriff Harvey A. Capron said his deputies would be stopping violators and asking them to slow down.

"Higher speeds aren't illegal, but they're not loyal," he said.

A three-week drive collected more than 100 tons of scrap rubber

Above: In 1944 Mary Vincent, 1717 Francis St., gazes at a treasured photograph of her son, John Vincent, Navy seaman second class. Right: Shirley Burdick bakes a cake to ship to her sons, Willard and Robert Burdick, both sergeants in the Army.

David McGill gets some shut-eye while trying to read the Jackson Citizen Patriot newspaper. McGill was exhausted after working 60-hour weeks at Macklin Co., 2914 Wildwood Ave. Flanking him are pictures of his sons, left, Navy Petty Officer First Class Donald McGill and Army Pfc. Gerald McGill.

— everything from rubber bands to overshoes to truck tires. One woman was said to have pried the rubber tips from the bottoms of her high heels. Jackson's contribution of 2.2 pounds of rubber per person was well above the U.S. average, according to officials.

In a highly symbolic gesture, the first Goodyear tire produced in Jackson was unchained from the floor in the office of the Greater Jackson Association and turned over to the military.

Along with it went a note from Ben Price, executive secretary of the association, to Leon Henderson, head of the U.S. Office of Price Administration.

"With the critical shortage of tires and rubber, this tire should be put to service in the war effort," Price wrote.

Young Jackson women got into the war effort in a big way by organizing a chapter of the Fort Custer Military Service Clubs.

The chapter's initial goal of 100 members was filled almost overnight, and 105 of them left for Battle Creek on June 9, 1942, to attend a dance for servicemen.

"Sweaters are taboo and the girls can't go bare-legged," said a newspaper report at the time. "Too-short skirts that swirl a bit too freely are frowned on, no matter how attractive. Rolled socks are banned."

The women paid their own way to Battle Creek by bus to be "assorted among the soldiers according to sizes and types," the newspaper said.

In every way, Jackson was a ➡

An unidentified woman holds on to the first Goodyear tire produced in Jackson in 1937. The tire was later released from the main office and donated to the war effort.

Gloria Horning decks out in a hula costume sent from her cousin, Sherman Johnson, who was stationed with the Army in Hawaii during the war.

Carroll Abrams, 11, smiles for a school photo in 1943. Carroll's family moved from Detroit that year when her father got a job in Jackson. She attended West Intermediate School.

Leona Lee and her daughter Marjorie, left, join Dorothy Lee Bausano and her little girl for some companionship on Easter 1943. Both of their husbands, Staff Sgt. Phillip Lee and Pfc. Charlie Bausano, were away serving with the Army Air Force.

community focused on winning the war.

In a 19-part series published in February 1943, the Jackson Citizen Patriot explored "the conversion of peacetime establishments to war production."

The newspaper found 17,000 people, including 3,700 women, employed in 76 war plants. One plant, which was unnamed, employed 30 people in June 1941. In February 1943 it employed 1,000.

Among the parts made in Jackson were airplane starters, wheels, brakes, self-sealing fuel tanks, radio equipment, axles, fans, bomb hoists, and machined and metal parts.

Also shells, shell cases, ammunition boxes, cannons, mufflers, wrenches, cranks, portable landing mats, gears,

War could not kill romance. A dreamy postcard envisions a kiss "across 10,000 miles." The card was locally printed by Miller Inc., 125 W. Michigan Ave.

Billye Freeman, wife of Army Cpl. T/5 J.W. "Jay" Freeman, stands on the front steps of the family home, 635 Kennedy St. She is holding daughter, Glenna, who was just a few months old when the soldier was drafted.

oxygen bottles, and refrigeration and air-conditioning equipment.

Also signals and sirens, landing gear signals, airplane mooring devices, bomb releases, machine-gun solenoids, automatic radio compasses and radio antennae.

Factories operated 24 hours a day, seven days a week.

The nation's manufacturing of warplanes, tanks, ships, trucks, cannons, guns and ammunition far surpassed the abilities of all of its enemies combined.

It wasn't easy, however. The strains of creating a 7 million man military, while at the same time finding personnel to operate the machines and factories, were evident throughout the economy.

The results were shortages, rationing, price controls and a horrendous toll in accidents. While U.S. war casualties by Sept. 30, 1943, had reached 115,000, including 22,000 killed, the National Safety Council said 7 million Americans had been injured in accidents, including 80,000 killed.

The rockets' red glare, bombs bursting in air came to Jackson in August 1943.

The occasion was a mock battle staged at the Jackson County Fairgrounds by four companies of the 792nd MP Battalion. The program was billed as the Army's "Salute to Agriculture, Industry and Labor."

The soldiers set up camp on the Ella Sharp Park baseball fields, where they were besieged by youngsters climbing over tanks, mock-driving Jeeps and handling the weapons of war. ➡

Jeffrey Reynolds, 2, dons a military hat and toy gun to copy his Army father, Donald A. Reynolds.

Kenneth Hayden, 5, is too young to join the Navy, but he can sure dress the part.

Ten-year-old Shirley Gebhardt, left, helps Kay Jennings, 3, ride a tricycle. The children were at a going-away party for Leonard Gebhardt, who was leaving for the Navy.

Betty Jensen, left, and sister Barbara Jensen say goodbye to the family dog before heading off to school in 1942.

Carol Ann Ide, left, and Betty Jensen try on their skates in August 1944. The girls were headed to the Rollatorium, 218 W. Ganson St.

"If the Army's equipment can stand the manhandling it's getting from these youngsters, it can take most anything," the Citizen Patriot suggested in reporting on the event.

Thousands of Jacksonians walked through the camp at the park, and thousands of others viewed a parade and an exhibit strung out along Jackson Street of products made in Jackson defense industries.

But the big show was at the fairgrounds, where 25,000 gathered for a mock battle narrated by Maj. Wayne King, otherwise known as "the Waltz King" and one of "America's outstanding orchestra leaders."

The battle began with attackers and defenders at opposite ends of the fairgrounds.

A scout patrol from the attackers spotted "tanks," three derelict automobiles. Using a "handy-talkie," (wired to the fairgrounds loudspeaker system) the Signal Corps, new 6-pound, hand-held radio, the scouts called for artillery support.

The attackers opened up with a 75-mm cannon and a 105-mm howitzer. The first shot fell short and the second was long. Adjustments were made, and the next shots blew the jalopies apart.

That was followed by a brisk firefight with rifles, machine guns and tommy guns, with shots punctuated by mortar blasts. As bombs, shells and land mines exploded, some soldiers pitched forward and lay still, as if dead.

Soon three tanks moved forward, racing through exploding land mines to squash the derelict automobiles.

The show was followed by a playing of the national anthem while the crowd roared its appreciation.

Jackson exploded in a joyous celebration on Aug. 14, 1945, when Japan announced its surrender.

Horn-honking automobiles packed Michigan Avenue from Ganson Street to Wildwood Avenue, the "circuit" favored in later years by teenage cruisers.

People clung to the sides, tops and fenders of cars as they worked their way through the crowded streets. Showers of torn-up newspapers, books, magazines, bathroom tissue and waste paper rained on citizens who came out of the stores and homes to join the revelry.

The wild demonstration and "terrific din" lasted for seven hours, until the exhausted citizens drifted home to bed. Reports were that the bell on St. John Catholic Church rang for 30 minutes, until it stuck in an upside-down position and couldn't ring anymore.

Police said 15 people were jailed and 13 were injured in traffic accidents.

Most Jackson factories, stores, bars and service stations remained closed over the next two days, in keeping with a holiday declared by President Harry S. Truman.

Even before the war ended, Jackson citizens were being prepared for a vastly different world then they had experienced for four years.

On Aug. 11, the Army and Navy announced cancellation of war contracts totaling $4 billion, threatening the jobs of 5 million munitions makers within 60 days. The Navy followed that announcement with the cancellation of 95 new ships, including a battleship and two aircraft carriers.

Within two weeks of the war's end, some 2,287 of Jackson's 12,885 defense plant workers had been laid off. Peace time had begun. ★

An American Red Cross class of nurses' aides receive their caps Dec. 1, 1943. The women were trained because of nursing shortages at Foote and Mercy hospitals.
They are, front row, left to right: Jean Dalton, Janice Steinke, Virginia Mosher, instructor Vera Platt, Patricia Terry, Joyce Ann Reed and Virginia Wissman.
Middle row, left to right: Frances Walicki, Shirley Reed, Patricia Seybold, Miriam Whitelock, Jane Zinc, Margaret Gilbert and Mary Bretes.
Top row, left to right: Margaret Goodacre, Virginia Brower, Enid Howard, Mary Smeenge, Georgia Bell, Helen Vaughn and Mary Lincoln.

Delaine Rose Hudson studies to become a nurse in 1943 in response to the nursing shortage. She studied for three years at Mercy Hospital's school of nursing and graduated in 1946.

Red Cross volunteers make light of the tough times in 1942. Enjoying the moment are, from left, Betty Cotton, Helen Cotton, Tom Riley, Jean Browning and Mary Ann Forner.

"Knit for Victory" promoted knitting as a way to show patriotism. The 15-page booklet cost 10 cents and featured directions for hats, socks, sweaters, mufflers and other warm items.

Every Monday at American Red Cross headquarters, members of the 119th Field Artillery Mothers' Club met to sew items all day. The group includes, standing left to right: Vida Salsig, Anna Embury, Ann Bosca, Genevieve Hasbrouck and Marie Kemmer.
Seated middle row, left to right are: Martha Millerlile, Ellen Worden, Mary Gamble, Mrs. H.C. Rex, Irene Olthouse, Mrs. A.J. Gee, Garnetta Grimes and Mrs. George Davis. Seated front at sewing machines are, left, Alva Clore and Freda Poling.

Victoria Fryt heads off to work at the Michigan Central Railroad while other family members serve in the armed forces.

The Hayes Wheel newsletter carries an official government insignia awarded to civilian factories. The Army-Navy "E" is awarded for outstanding production of war materials.

Four women in the Hayes Industries Inc. inspection department dress alike to show a united war effort. The workers are, from left, Maxine Ross, Ellen Zaski, Dorothy Chadderton and Thelma Purfield.

Six Konkol sisters ride their bikes to work at Goodyear Tire & Rubber Co. Plant guard James Tester gives clearance to, left to right: Betty, showing her badge; Clara; Anne; Virginia; Margaret; and Agnes. The women filled some of the vacancies created when more than 300 workers left to serve in the armed forces.

Joyce M. Smith goes to work at the Jackson Crankshaft plant on E. Michigan Avenue. Smith ran a grinder that smoothed the ends off tank pins. Her husband, Pfc. Fred J. Smith, was serving in the Army.

Margaret Strickrodt Kulchinski goes to work in 1942 at McLellan's, a dime-store located at 149 W. Michigan Ave.

Norma Baker, left, and Evelyn Markiewicz take a break while working at the Homade Food Market, 188-190 W. Michigan Ave. Baker staffed the luncheon counter, and Markiewicz was a hostess.

John Kuhl gets out from behind the Homade Food Market meat counter. Kuhl stands in the N. Jackson Street alley next to Casler Hardware and the former post office building.

The Jackson Citizen Patriot promoted war bonds using profiles of local servicemen. The hand-drawn advertising featured the soldiers' families, former jobs and hobbies.

Staff Sgt. Guy Robert Champney of the Army Air Corps

Army Pfc. John Kurpinski (Kurpenski)

Army Tech. 5 Duane Huntoon

Lt. Howard J. Lougheed of the Army Air Corps

Fred Rosa works at a bench at Frost Gear & Forge, a division of Clark Equipment Co., located at S. Horton and Tyson streets. Rosa worked seven days a week at the factory supplying war parts.

Oscar T. Rice mans a machine at Frost Gear & Forge on Tyson Street. Many companies experienced a shortage of factory workers during the war.

113

The General Products shop committee displays the coveted Army-Navy "E" flag, awarded to companies who met government war-production standards. Left to right are: Lyle Houghton, Bert Pontius, Bill Smith, Virgil Keller, Chuck Langham, Rex Linsner and Al Peters.

A General Products April 6, 1945, newsletter encourages workers to keep up the production of war materials.

Blanche Wilson Vinton works on horns at the Sparks-Withington Co. plant on W. North Street.

A large "V" for victory lists an honor roll of Sparks-Withington Co. employees who had joined the armed forces. The sign was displayed in front of the horn plants on W. North Street.

General Products Corp. workers make shell, bomb and rocket parts for the government. By August 1942, the entire plant's facilities at 103 N. Horton St. were devoted to war work.

An unidentified Goodyear worker is surrounded by women selling bonds outside the tire plant. From left, Barbara Wilson, Virginia Mandreger and Jane Best try to convince the man to buy.

Sparks-Withington's Co.'s "Save and Serve for Victory" committee plans a war-bond rally to be held May 14, 1942, at Jackson High School auditorium.

The 1944 Jackson High School band performs a concert as part of the local bond effort. Arnold Waltz and Gloria Horning play their instruments from the second row on the left, first and second chairs.

The Sparton Bombshell, the in-house newsletter at Sparks-Withington Corp., pushes war bonds as a great savings plan for children.

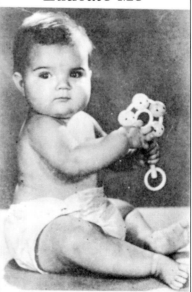

War Bonds Will Educate Me

This young man's smart mother and dad are putting all the money possible in to War Bonds. Ten or fifteen years from now it will cost them just three fourths as much to educate junior as it would otherwise, for every $3.00 invested brings a return of $4.00 from Uncle Sam.

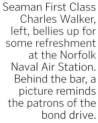

Seaman First Class Charles Walker, left, bellies up for some refreshment at the Norfolk Naval Air Station. Behind the bar, a picture reminds the patrons of the bond drive.

Above: Yeoman Second Class Thomas R. Hawkins sells war bonds in March 1945 to a ship's barber at the Naval Air Station in Minneapolis, Minn.
Right: Colorful bond posters tout the need "to pull together" so America could win the war.

Navy Machinist Mate Second Class Warren Niles Bennett sports two war bonds to promote sales. For every month he served in the Pacific, Bennett purchased $100 worth of bonds.

A Railway Express Agency truck parks in Jackson in 1943 to promote the 3rd War Loan drive. "Back the Attack!" was the bond slogan.

A parade moves east on E. Michigan Avenue during a 1943 war-bond promotion.

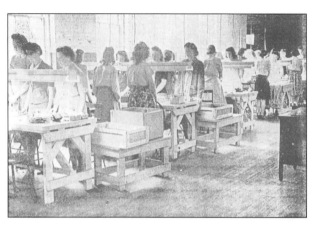

The employees of Sparks-Withington Co., Plant 5, 2301 E. Michigan Ave., stop for prayer at 10 a.m. June 6, 1944. Church bells chimed citywide to signal a moment of meditation on D-Day, the start of the invasion of France.

Pedestrians and traffic come to a standstill on E. Michigan Avenue on June 6, 1944, at 10 a.m. during a citywide minute of meditation during the D-Day invasion.

A group of students enters St. John Catholic Church, 717 Cooper St., to pray on D-Day, June 6, 1944, the beginning of the Allied Forces' invasion of Normandy, France.

Army Tech. 5 Bill Goudie checks the mirror, making sure he looks good for the Christmas holiday.

Army Sgt. Clayton McNaughton drums up some attention at his home at 612 Milwaukee St.

Navy Seaman First Class Raymond Boleslaw Majchrowski walks along the 100 block of E. Michigan Avenue while on his one and only leave. Majchrowski joined the Navy at 17 and was killed Oct. 26, 1942, while serving on the USS Aircraft Carrier Hornet. The ship was sunk in the Battle of Santa Cruz islands.

Army Cpl. William J. Hampton gets some cautionary advice in April 1943 from an important family member, Treve the dog.

Howard Mallett stands in his Army uniform in front of a Spring Arbor home. Mallett served in the Home Guard and later died from complications of scarlet fever.

Right: Army Pvt. John R. Gage stands proudly on his own, using a cane, on his 20th birthday, Dec. 24, 1945. Gage was celebrating at his home on John Street in Parma. He was originally told after a spinal-cord injury that he would never walk again. Far right: Gage, on crutches, accepts a bet he can't make it up the hill at a picnic for recovering soldiers. Gage was at the Gull Lake annex of Percy Jones Hospital in Kalamazoo County.

Army Air Force Sgt. Robert Wellman sticks his head out of the Abraham Lincoln Hotel in Springfield, Ill. Wellman stayed there in 1943 while picking up some equipment.

Franklin "Jim" Tilford, center, finishes up his ski run on Mount Rainier on Dec. 7, 1941. Tilford was kicked off the slopes because of the attack on Pearl Harbor. He was drafted into the Army and became a major.

Jim Feeny of the Army likes having the chance to drive around Jackson while home on leave on April 12, 1945.

Staff Sgt. Phillip J. Lee sports a bomber jacket while serving as a tailgunner with the Army Air Force. The markings on the right chest represent each enemy plane he shot down.

A Western Union telegram informs the mother of Pfc. Fred Vinton of his rescue from a Japanese prisoner-of-war camp. The Marine was released Jan. 30, 1945.

Marine Pfc. Fred S. Vinton returns to Sparks-Withington Co. to say hello to his former co-workers. Vinton was released Jan. 30, 1945, from a Japanese prisoner-of-war camp.

Army Pfc. John Bryan puts an arm around his mother, Ethel Bryan, while at home on leave in September 1943.

Perry Lake of the Navy spends some time outside with mother Margaret Lake during a 1944 furlough.

Tech. 5 Sgt. Cleo Harold Lorencen spends time with his mother, Mary Gray Lorencen, while he was stationed in California with the Army.

Cora Otto goes outside her Condad Street house April 26, 1944, to talk with her son, Army Sgt. Charles Maynard Otto.

Army Tech. 5 John K. Kohn shares a hug with his mother, Agnes Kohn, in 1942 at their home on Mount Hope Road. Kohn could not share anything about his recent training involving a secret technology called radar.

In 1943, Army Air Force Lt. Col. Claude Spencer gets some advice from his mother, Abbie Kalmbach, at the family homestead at 669 S. Sutton Road.

Army Cpl. Burton Richardson, left, catches up with his family Sept. 3, 1944, at 614 Orange St. Mother Bernice Richardson dons a sailor cap from her other son, Robert "Bubs" Richardson, who had just finished boot camp. "Bubs" later rose to Navy machinist mate third class.

Homecoming day, Oct. 29, 1945, is celebrated by Frances Glinicki, Army Sgt. Willard Burdick, and his parents, Shirley and Elon Burdick. Burdick served with the 2nd Calvary, Patton's 3rd Army in Europe.

Army Air Corps Staff Sgt. Louis L. Ratkiewicz stops by 307 Cooper St. to visit with his foster parents, Harold and Edna Boland. Ratkiewicz started his military career with the Royal Canadian Air Force and later moved to the American forces.

Army Air Corps Sgt. Floyd Doherty, left, spends some time with his parents, Cora and Harry Doherty.

Navy Electrician Mate First Class Philip Farrand sits on the coach with his parents, Edna and Edward Farrand, during a leave home.

Cpl. Dennis Ernie Reynolds enjoys leave before heading to England with the Army Air Force. Reynolds is with his parents, Olive and Harold Reynolds.

The Budd family has a get-together in 1942 after basic training for Navy Petty Officer First Class Richard Budd. Budd, left, is joined by mother Ellen; brother Walter Budd Jr., tender third class of the Coast Guard; and father, Walter Budd.

The McInerney parents share leave time in 1942 with both sons. From left are Army Major Vincent M. McInerney, mother Mary, father Martin, and Army Air Force Staff Sgt. Thomas S. McInerney.

Astoria, N.Y., was a great place in 1945 for a shore leave for Don Shewman, Navy torpedoman's mate second class, and his fiancée, Marie Imp.

Sharp Park is a special place for Roberta Lincoln and Navy coxswain Leonard Gebhardt. The couple enjoy a date Sept. 10, 1943, before Gebhardt ships out to Europe.

Cpl. Louis O'Connell and his date, USO entertainer Mary Lee, enjoy an evening talk. O'Connell was stationed in the Aleutian Islands in 1943 with the Army's 119th Field Artillery.

Tech. 5 Earl L. Hill and fiancée, Ida R. Sanford, spend some time together in Jackson before he shipped out. The couple tied the knot April 4, 1943, in Abilene, Texas, just before the Army sent Hill to Europe.

James M. Richardson, Navy seaman second class, enjoys an April 1944 weekend in Chicago with his girlfriend, Penny. The sailor later got a tattoo emblazoned with her name.

Jean Herdus and Pvt. Paul Chmielewski walk through a military guard of honor at their wedding. The couple were married July 7, 1945, at St. Stanislaus Catholic Church. Chmielewski was a former German prisoner-of-war, imprisoned at Munich for a year.

2nd Lt. Richard Zeller and wife Pauline repeat their marriage vows before family and friends in a church wedding April 1945 at the Spring Arbor College chapel. The couple had wed earlier Feb. 3, 1945, in Jacksonville, Fla. The judge was late, so the civil ceremony was performed at 11 p.m. Pauline had originally flown down for a short visit. The pair decided to get married so she could permanently stay while Richard served in the Marines.

William and Delfina Cintron Wineland pose as man and wife after their 1945 wedding. Wineland served as a corporal in the Army infantry.

Margaret Glaspie and Cleo Harold Lorencen met around Valentine's Day 1942 at Wilson's Service Station. Six weeks later, Lorencen joined the Army. The couple were married on July 7, 1943.

The wedding day for Lloyd Kabel and Ruth Comstock was July 29, 1945. Kabel was a Tech. 5 with the Army.

Louise Mary McIntosh and T/Sgt. W.B. "Pete" Caldwell join in marriage March 22, 1945. Caldwell had returned after serving with the Army Air Force in the South Pacific.

1st Sgt. James Kenneth McConnell met Lillian Marie Hager at a USO dance while stationed with the Army at Fort Leonard Wood, Mo. The couple later took their vows on Aug. 1, 1943, in Jefferson City, Mo.

Leona Stout Leffler and Pvt. Chester W. Leffler pose in 1944 for a portrait. Chester presented Leona with a $75 engagement ring as a Christmas gift in 1941. They wed June 26, 1943.

Aleck and Alice Mandreger enjoy some at-home time in March 1944. Mandreger flew as a bombardier while serving as a staff sergeant in the Army Air Force.

Pvt. Warren A. Dexter and his wife, Neva E., enjoy a short break in October 1943 after basic training in Macon, Ga. Dexter shipped out after the leave. Dexter later served as a sergeant in Army Company F, 143rd Infantry, Texas 36th Division, that moved on foot from southern Italy to France.

Lt. Howard Robb and his wife, Norma, enjoy a night in Jackson at a banquet. Robb was a pilot for the Army Air Force Air Transport Wing. He flew B-24s and CB-24s and earned the Distinguished Flying Cross and Air Medal.

Janet and Edwin "Joe" Schaffer talk on the steps of their home. The couple married before Schaffer's Navy boot camp. The chief petty officer was assigned to the Ticonderoga CV14 in the South Pacific.

Charlotte Bennett Buckles cuddles next to Navy Motor Machinist Mate First Class Harold Ross Buckles in 1945 during a furlough home.

Doris Dickerson, right, introduces 15-month-old Julie Dickerson to her father, George A. Dickerson. The Army Air Force second lieutenant was meeting his daughter for the first time on Father's Day, June 13, 1945.

Navy Yeoman Second Class Thomas R. Hawkins, center, visits with his wife, Marjorie, and children, Tom, left, Wendy and Betsy in 1944.

Army Pvt. Donald Reynolds, right, stands outside his parents' home on Cortland Boulevard with his son, Jeffrey, and wife, Millie, while home on leave October 1944.

The living room is a happy reunion spot for the Ralph Dimmick family. From left are, Ralph's mother, Mabel Dimmick; Army 1st Sgt. Ralph Dimmick Sr. with niece Sandy Wineland on lap; children Ralph Jr. and Clara; wife Mary Brush Dimmick; and Pearl Dimmick Wineland holding Sue Wineland.

Army Air Corps Staff Sgt. Phillip J. Lee takes time in November 1944 to get a professional family photo before shipping out to go overseas to Italy. With him is his wife, Leona, and his daughter, Marjorie.

The Fritz family of Spring Arbor gathers for a formal family photo. Standing in back, left to right, are Arnold, David, Viola, Hugh and Tazwell Fritz. Seated in front are parents Susie and Jesse Fritz.

Charles VanAkin poses with his family Dec. 22, 1943, on Elizabeth Street in Parma before heading out to Army boot camp. Standing right of Charles is his wife, Marian. In the front are daughters Margene, left, and Nancy. VanAkin served as a private first class.

Henry D. Leigh, 4, salutes his uncle, Capt. Stuart R. Leigh, while wearing his borrowed military cap. The Marine pilot was home on leave at his parents' house at 2614 Francis St.

Marine Sgt. Chester Young, center, gathers around his favorite girls, mother Leola Young, left, wife Catherine Young, and 4-year-old Patricia Young.

Dennis Ross Buckles drags his uncle, Army Air Corps T/Sgt. Gordon Nathaniel Bennett, out on the porch in 1943 for some one-on-one time.

Navy Aviation Boatswain's Mate First Class Edward Augustine, right, hangs on to Annette Kramic while sharing a 1943 visit with Tony Augustine, left, and Ann Kramic.

Above: Army Pfc. Alfred Konkol bounces his nephew David Zakrzewski on his lap while checking out the family farm in Parma. Left: Army Pfc. Sherman Berkeypile holds baby brother, Donald Berkeypile, at the family home on Palmer Road in Brooklyn. On the back step, Delbert Berkeypile picks a guitar while Albert Berkeypile plays the harmonica.

Army Tech. 5 Leo Pec stands in front of his Russell Street home with mother Pauline Pec and niece Judy Vincent. Pec received an honorable discharge on his 27th birthday — Oct. 31, 1945.

Navy Seaman 1st Class Leonard Joseph Schweda, right, squats down to hear a message from his little brother, Gerald Schweda.

Ten-year-old Connie McGill, left, and Johnny McGill, 8, are excited to be with brother Donald McGill, Navy chief petty officer first class. The sailor was on a June 1942 furlough. McGill later suffered severe burns in an air crash in the South Pacific.

Seaman Second Class Robert L. Freeman gets support from his nephews, all wearing Navy sailor suits. Freeman stands in back holding 1-year-old George R. "Butch" Freeman. In front, left to right, are Albert Curtiss, 3; Donald Curtiss, 5; and Richard Curtiss, 7.

Family gathers around Pfc. Gerald McGill, back left. Standing center is mother Pearl McGill by father David McGill. In front are siblings Johnny and Connie, holding Dewey the cat. The Army soldier served three years with the military police in London and Belgium.

Nick Luppo, Navy seaman first class, second from left, enjoys a home visit with brother Charlie, left, and parents Joseph and Josephine Luppo.

The Winelands pose for a family picture during a 1945 visit in Brooklyn. Army Pvt. William Wineland is joined by brother Leroy Wineland, left, Pearl Wineland and nephew Walter Wineland.

Donald Smith, right, gets a warm send-off on a cold February day in 1942 from brother Gordon Smith and sister Elsa Knight. Smith stopped at the County Farm Road family home before leaving for Army basic training at Fort Custer. Smith served as a private first class.

Four Hendrick brothers share some leave time. They are left to right, Army soldiers Rollin Hendrick and Charles Hendrick; Seabee Gordon Hendrick, Navy fireman first class electrician mate construction battalion; and Army Cpl. Ival Hendrick.

Navy Chief Petty Officer Second Class Keith Porlier gives some brotherly advice in 1945 to Elaine Porlier at the family's home at 922 S. Sutton Road.

Sophie and Ted Czubko share a brother-sister visit at 2729 Cooper St. Pfc. Ted Czubko served in the Army Air Force in the South Pacific.

Navy Seaman First Class Nick Luppo enjoys a chuckle with his cousin, Grace Bionda.

In 1945, all Augustine brothers get together in their old eastside neighborhood at Page Avenue and Johnson Street. From left are Joseph Augustine, Frank Augustine in the Army, Tony Augustine, Walter Augustine in the Army, Army Pfc. Benny Augustine, John Augustine in the Navy and Army Pfc. Stanley Augustine.

Edward Bryant, left, of the Navy visits his East Jackson High School classmate Navy Electrician Mate Third Class Norman Ulrich. The sailors missed their senior year to serve on separate LST ships in the Pacific. Although they missed graduation, they later received diplomas.

Navy buddies Ensign Henry J. Konkol, left, and Petty Officer Third Class William "Red" Hoffman enjoy a 1945 spring day at the Konkols' Benn Road farm in Parma.

Emmet Schell takes a moment during a family visit in 1945 to talk with nephew Army Air Corps T/Sgt. Gordon Bennett.

Navy Seaman Second Class Raymond B. Zakrzewski, right, and his brother, Thadeusz S. Zakrzewski, also of the Navy, share family stories and cold refreshments.

Army Air Corps Master Sgt. Lozell Jordon and his brother, Navy Fireman First Class Clare "Stub" Jordon, enjoy the lucky opportunity of getting home leave at the same time in 1942.

Army Air Corps Staff Sgt. Charles Edward Scott has a warm visit — despite the snow — with his hometown friend Charles Sierakis, also of the Army Air Corps.

The home of Army Tech. 5 Bill Goudie, 915 Westwood Blvd., is a gathering spot in July 1945 for other Army soldiers. Goudie, left, "Teato" Whitlow and Allyn Wright goof around while home on leave.

Army Sgt. Kenneth Hoch, seated left, enjoys a sandwich with some friends while on leave in 1943 from Camp Howze, Texas. Hoch grabbed a bus and spent a weekend in Dallas.

A May 1943 visit home allows cousins Wayne Whitlock, right, an Army military police officer, and Army Pfc. Otis Whitlock an opportunity to share family stories.

Staff Sgt. Aleck Mandreger, right, shares his experiences as a bombardier with an Army Air Force buddy.

Marine Pvt. Chuck Kulchinski, right, visits his W. Monroe Street neighbor, William Strickrodt, while home in 1943.

Checking out their old stomping grounds at Jackson High School are former classmates and Army soldiers Owen Johnson, right, and Tech. 5 Bill Goudie.

Brothers Pvt. Rex Beach Bennett of the Army and Warren Niles Bennett, Navy aviation machinist mate second class, rendezvous in Hawaii while on leave in 1944.

Navy Torpedoman's Mate Second Class Don Shewman, right, didn't land the big one, but still has a great day fishing. Shewman shows off a large catch of bluegills he pulled out of a lake near Cement City with an unidentified friend.

Good times still happen for three former Jackson High School classmates. Clowning around by Johnson Brothers Pharmacy, 420 First St., are Navy sailor Doug Raymer, who holds Army Tech. 5 Bill Goudie. Army buddy Owen Johnson hangs on to Goudie's legs.

Awards

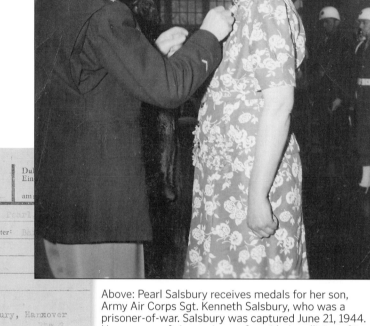

Above: Pearl Salsbury receives medals for her son, Army Air Corps Sgt. Kenneth Salsbury, who was a prisoner-of-war. Salsbury was captured June 21, 1944. He was one of six survivors of a mid-air collision of two B-17 bombers.

Left: Salsbury's German prisoner-of-war papers show his pictures, fingerprints and other identifying marks. Salsbury became a POW after his B-17 bomber crashed near Rheineberg, Germany. Four of the crew were captured and six were killed. The document was given to him at the time of his release.

Dulag-Luft. Kriegsgefangenenkartei.

NAME:	S A L S B U R Y
Vornamen:	Kenneth L.
Dienstgrad:	Sgt. Funktion: Günner
Matrikel-No.:	36 459 197
Geburtstag:	4.9.24
Geburtsort:	Jackson, Michigan
Religion:	Prot.
Zivilberuf:	Farmer
Staatsangehörigkeit:	USA.

Gefangenen-Erkennungsmarke: Luftwaff Nr. 2742

Vorname des Vaters: Pearl
Familienname der Mutter:
Verheiratet mit:
Anzahl der Kinder:

Heimatanschrift:
Mr. P. J. Salsbury, Hanover
Michigan.

Abschluß am: 21.6.44 bei: Berlin
Gefangennahme am: wie oben bei: Rheinsberg

Flugzeugtyp: B 17

Nähere Personalbeschreibung

Figur:	groß	Augen:	braun
Größe:	1.79	Nase:	kurz u. dick
Schädelform:	oval	Bart:	ohne
Haare:	braun	Gebiß:	gesund
Gewicht:	72 kg		
Gesichtsform:	voll	Besondere Kennzeichen:
Gesichtsfarbe:	braun	Blinddarmnarbe.

Front   Profil   Fingerabdruck

Rechter Zeigefinger

The European-African-Middle Eastern Campaign Medal is awarded to any military personnel serving between Dec. 7, 1941, and March 2, 1946, in Europe, North Africa or the Middle East. The colored bands represent Germany, on the ribbon's right: Italy, on its left; and the United States, in the center.

The Asiatic-Pacific Campaign Medal was created Nov. 6, 1942, by Franklin D. Roosevelt to recognize any U.S. military member who served in the Pacific Theater from Dec. 7, 1941, to March 2, 1946. There were 21 official Army and 48 Navy/Marine campaigns.

Above: Marine Pfc. Russell Webb Anderson receives his Purple Heart. Anderson was wounded in the hip by shrapnel Sept. 15, 1944, while fighting in the Palau group in the Pacific.
Left: Capt. Michael awards Warren Niles Bennett, Navy aviation machinist mate second class, a Distinguished Flying Cross. The Sept. 5, 1944, ceremony was conducted aboard the USS Cabot aircraft carrier on tour in the Pacific. Bennett was injured while parachuting from a burning plane that was hit by ack-ack near Yap Island.

Electrician Mate First Class Harold E. Casler, owner of Casler Hardware, receives a special award at the Naval Training School in Lafayette, Ind. Casler earned a 3.9 out of 4.0 score, the highest rating ever achieved by a trainee.

The American Campaign Medal was created Nov. 6, 1942, by Franklin D. Roosevelt to recognize military personnel who performed service in the American Theater of Operation during World War II. The region was defined as the continental United States including most of the Atlantic Ocean, a portion of Alaska, and a small piece of the Pacific bordering California and Baja, California.

The World War II Victory Medal was authorized July 6, 1945, by an Act of Congress and awarded to all military personnel for service between Dec. 7, 1941, and Dec. 31, 1946.

Sgt. Louis J. Ratkiewicz shakes hands with his commanding officer. Ratkiewicz served with the Royal Canadian Air Force after being rejected by the Army Air Corps because of teeth problems. Ratkiewicz later moved to the Army Air Corps as a staff sergeant.

Coming home

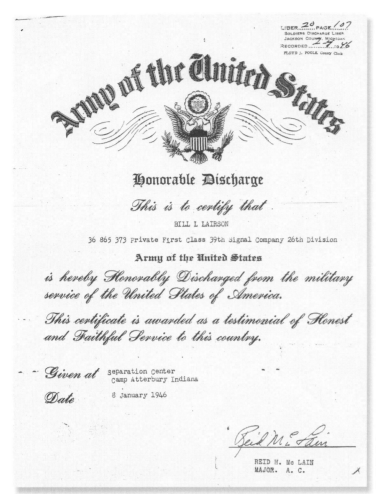

The Ruptured Duck was an insignia depicting an eagle inside a wreath. It was worn on uniforms above the right breast pocket by World War II servicemen and women. It was issued to those who were about to leave the military with an Honorable Discharge. It allowed them to continue to wear their uniform for up to 30 days, since there was a clothing shortage at that time. This showed they were in transit and not AWOL.

The nickname came from the popular notion that the eagle looked more like a duck and, because they were going home, "They took off like a Ruptured Duck."

Army Pfc. Bill L. Lairson's honorable discharge papers contain a certificate and a detailed record of his military career, including battle and campaigns, decorations and dates of service.

Army Air Corps T/Sgt. Max Hotchkin was one of thousands aboard the Marine Jumper in 1945, returning to the States after the war. The newly built ship carried troops from China, Burma and India.

"Going back to civilian life" was a government booklet issued by the War Department to all discharged personnel of the Army. It explained veterans' rights and gave suggestions for going back to families and former jobs.

The Aug. 14, 1945, Jackson Citizen Patriot announces the end of the war. The special edition hit the streets by 7 p.m., less than one hour after Japan's surrender.

The streets of downtown Jackson are jammed with people and cars August 14, 1945, V-J Day. The celebration started shortly after 6 p.m. and continued until dawn.

Army Pfc. Clark Winchell sailed home on the Webster Victory, a cargo ship that sailed from Le Havre, France. Five hundred thirty-four Victory ships were built during the war to replace the huge losses of vessels due to German submarines.

Fred Rosa, second from right, raises his arms and cheers along with his fellow workers at Frost Gear & Forge on Tyson Street. The group just heard the news of victory over Germany on May 8, 1945. The plant's operation was halted to celebrate.

USS Cape Perpetua enters Puget Sound en route to Seattle. The transport ship was bringing soldiers back from Japan in November 1945. Lt. Chris Davis was aboard as a crew member for the Merchant Marines.

UNITED STATES COAST GUARD

DETROIT COAST GUARD BASE
3760 E. Jefferson Ave.
Detroit 7, Michigan

16 March, 1944

Mr. Arthur L. Gee
612 Homewild Avenue
Jackson, Michigan

Dear Mr. Gee:

The Navy Department and Commandant U. S. Coast Guard express sincere regrets that your son William Arthur Gee, R.M.3c. is missing in action with the enemy in the North Atlantic on 9 March, 1944.

Allotments for support of dependents and payments of insurance premiums will continue in effect. In order to prevent possible aid to the enemy it is requested that you do not divulge the name of the ship your son was on.

W. E. CHAPO, Lieutenant
Acting Commanding Officer
Detroit Coast Guard Base

A letter addressed to Arthur L. Gee contains bad news: Your son is missing in action. Coast Guard Seaman Second Class William Arthur Gee, left, was killed March, 9, 1944, when a German submarine torpedoed the USS Leopold, south of Iceland.

Sgt. Robert Wellman of the Army Air Force found time in July 1945 on Ie Shima to visit the site of Ernie Pyle's death. The Pulitzer Prize-winning reporter was killed by a Japanese machine-gun bullet to the left temple. The island is located off the west coast of Okinawa. A monument was immediately put on the site stating "At this spot, the 77th Infantry Division lost a buddy, Ernie Pyle 18 April, 1945."

Wellman also made a stop at Pyle's first grave, one of thousands on Ie Shima. The early cross marker used simple stenciling to note the site. The soldiers of the 77th made a wooden coffin for Pyle and buried him wearing his helmet. Later he was reburied at the Army cemetery on Okinawa and finally moved to the National Memorial Cemetery of the Pacific, Punchbowl Crater, located in Honolulu.

We remember those from Jackson County who died serving during World War II:

Pvt. Thomas Adams
T-5 Alver Anderberg
Cpl. Elmer C. Anderson
Pvt. Harold Appel
T-3 James J. Archambault
Kenneth Aten, WT 2-c
Pfc. Zygmunt Backus
Robert Baggs, S 1-C
Lt. Elwood Bailey
Pfc. Malcolm Bailey
Pfc. Arthur C. Bamm Jr.
Lt. William E. Barnes
Pfc. Benjamin F. Bean Jr.
Trpdmn 3-C Vern C. Beckwith Jr.
Cpl. William Belden
Lt. Robert Bentley
Seaman James Berry
Pfc. Theodore Berutko
Pfc. Gene Betts
Pvt. Vyrlan W. Birdsall
Lt. Frederick Bofink
Sgt. Charles Bonney
Pfc. Glenn E. Briggs
Btwn Mate 1-C Victor F. Brinkman
Cpl. Dean Brooks
Pfc. Otto J. Bruske
Pfc. Bernard Bucrek
Cpl. Verlin F. Burmis
2nd Lt. John T. Burns
Staff Sgt. Ralph P. Burns
Pvt. Curtis A. Buskirk
Lt. Edward Callahan
Pvt. Dale E. Campbell
Pvt. Daniel Carlsen
Cpl. Frank M. Carlson
Lt. Carl Carpenter
Pvt. Henry F. Carr
Lt. John L. Carter
A-C Bernard J. Cawley
Elmer Chaffin, F 1-c
Kenneth Chaffin, F 1-c
Arlo Chamberlain, MM 1-c
Pvt. Milton F. Chapin
Ensign Robert J. Chapman
Pvt. Martin Chossen
Pfc. Pete A. Christou
Gladyn Clark, AMM 3-c
Pt. Richard Cole
Pvt. Francis J. Conrath
Staff Sgt. James W. Cox
Pvt. George W. Crandall
Lt. Duane T. Crossthwaite
Pfc. Arthur Cumberworth
T-5 Floyd J. Cunningham

Pfc. Henry F. Czarnecki
Stanley Czarnecki, F 1-c
Staff Sgt. Mark Daniels
Sgt. Gerald Davis
A-C Homer J. Dees
Lt. Lawrence Degener
Albert W. Degutis, S 2-c
Capt. Jack M. Deming
Cpl. W. M. Dennis
Cpl. F. E. Deuel Jr.
Maj. Leland K. Dewey
Pvt. John Draganov
T-Sgt. Harold J. Dunham
Pfc. Edward S. Dzienis
Pfc. Philip Egan
Staff Sgt. Donald Eggleston
Pfc. Robert S. Ekin
Lt. Ralph Ellis
Staff Sgt. Arlo R. Emmerson
Sgt. James T. Etienne
Ensign Lawrence Faling
Cpl. Francis Ferguson
Capt. Walter R. Finton
Pvt. Roy Fishmeister
Sgt. Virgil Fleming
Lt. Hollis W. Forbes
Capt. Robert F. Forbes
Pfc. Ernest E. Fox
Pvt. Richard Fox
1st Lt. Carol M. Frang
Pvt. Harold Freeland
Staff Sgt. James R. Freiberg
Sgt. Richard J. Freundl
Pfc. Virgil H. Furlong
Pfc. Freddie Gallagos
Seaman 1-C Harold E. Gallihugh

Robert Bruce Gattshall, Coxswain
Lt. Frederick C. Gauss
Delvin C. Gaylord, E 2-c
William A. Gee, R 3-c
Pvt. Kenneth Gillies
Staff Sgt. Lorran Goodsell
Paul Gordon, SF 1-c
Pvt. Raymond Gordon
Lt. Fred J. Graf
Pvt. Neil D. Graham
Pfc. Edward H. Greenwood
Pfc. Duon Grief
Pfc. Robert J. Griffin
Pfc. Winthrop Grill
Pvt. Phillip R. Hastings
Pvt. Jack C. Haines
T-5 Maurice Heffner
Capt. Philip Heiler
W.C. Herndon, S 2-c
Pfc. Lavern E. Hiner
Pfc. Leon D. Hinkle
Pvt. Burnett Hobner
Pfc. Walter F. Hoch
Pfc. Kenneth L. Holderman
Pfc. Roscoe Holmes
Pvt. Ralph Hoover
Pfc. Ellis Horsfall
1st Lt. Jack Hourning
Lt. Norman J. Hunt
Lt. Winston W. Hunt
Sgt. Cyril Hudecheck
Sidney L. Jackson, S 1-c
Pvt. Paul Johnson
Pvt. Russell Johnson
Staff Sgt. Joseph R. Kelly
Sgt. Roy Kimbel

Okinawa's 1st Marine Division Cemetery in 1945, a few months after the battles. Army Pfc. Austin Ladd photographed the graves.

Pfc. Richard L. Kistka
Pvt. Harold T. Klinkman
Merlin H. Kloack, F 1-c
Pfc. Robert Klump
Cpl. Burl J. Knapp
George A. Kramer, S 1-c
Sgt. LaVerne C. Krugman
Pfc. Joseph J. Kuzma
Pvt. Delbert Lair
Leonard Lair SM 3-c
Arthur Isaac Lamb, CMM-CPO
Keith Lee
Cpl. Wilbur H. Lehman
Sgt. Fred Larocque
Pfc. Philip L. Lawler
Pvt. John Leviski
Larry Larson, F 1-c
A-C Howard C. Lincoln
Sgt. Orville Lee
Cpl. Zygie Machczynski
Raymond Majchrowski, S 1-c
Lt. Dean Margworth
Pfc. Edward J. Markiewicz
Pfc. Frank A. Marriott
Leroy W. Marsh, BM 2-c
T-5 Allen E. Marvin
Lt. Geoffery Matthews
T-5 Howard A. Maurer
Pvt. Richard N. Mayo
Pfc. Donald McClure
Morgan J. McConnell, S 1-c
Harry M. McDonough, USN
Lt. Dwight McNally
Sgt. George T. McQuillan
Pvt. Leonard Meek
Pvt. Robert Merrill
Henry J. Miller, CGM
Pfc. Dick Mills
Pvt. Hugh D. Moffatt
Pfc. Wayne H. Moore
T-5 Francis X. Moran
Sgt. Roland E. Morehouse
Pfc. Jerry C. Moulton
Duwayne Murray, F 2-c
Sgt. Ronald A. Meyers
Pfc Norman A. Nichols
Pfc. William E. Nichols
Pfc. Stanley Niciporek
Pvt. LeMone R. Norton
Staff Sgt. Jack O'Dowd
Pfc. Donald Oexler
Pvt. Raymond A. Osenbaugh
Pfc. Robert Overmyer
Lt. Bert H. Parks
Sgt. Adam Parzych
Pvt. Nicholas Perlos
Sgt. Jonas P. Peterson

Nancie Pett, ARC Nurse
Pfc. Donald Phelps
Staff Sgt. Gene R. Phelps
Pfc. Marshall Phelps
Keith E. Phend, USN
Pvt. Clyde M. Phillips
Pvt. Harry J. Pickering Jr.
Sgt. Arthur M. Plows
Lt. Arthur Z. Pond
Lt. Vernon A. Post
Pfc. William Patrick Powers
Pfc. Frank Puglise
Staff Sgt. Robert H. Raems
Pfc. Harold J. Raser
Pfc. John L. Rasmussen
Pfc. Paul Reardon
Pvt. Richard W. Reasner
Ensign Jack H. Redinger
Cpl. Donald Redmond
Pvt. Daniel M. Reid
Lt. Carroll R. Robinson
Tech. Sgt. Robert L. Reynolds
Capt. John Rubsam
Pvt. William James Rooney
Cpl. Ralph G. Russell
Pfc. William O. Russell
Ensign William T. Sackrider
Pfc. Raymond E. Sanders
Pfc. Leroy Sanford
Sgt Sigmund Sarata
Pvt. Theodore Schmidt
Donald L. Sharp
Robert P. Shredow, CM 20c
Pvt. Raymond E Simco
Pvt. Cleo T. Simon
Pvt. Albert Sines
Pvt. Leonard Sines
Sgt. W. Grant Smalley

Sgt. Vernon Smalley
Staff Sgt. E. J. Smith
Staff Sgt. Robert Stoddard
Pvt. William Stoddard
Pfc. Lee O. Storm
Pvt. Charles Straham
Cpl. Gerald R. Straw
Cpl. Robert W. Sutton
Pfc. Milburn Taylor
Sqdn. Cmdr. Russell F. Taylor
Sgt. Garth G. Thurston
Staff Sgt. Don C. Tuttle
Charles W. Vaughan, S 1-c
A-C James W. Vogel
A-C Donald R. Vrooman
Pfc. Ray L. Wagner
Edward J. Wasilewski, S 1-c
Staff Sgt. Gordon Waldron
Sgt. Jerome Watson
Pvt. William Watson
Staff Sgt. Wlliam J. Weber
T-4 Harold H. Werner
Orien R. Wetzel, F 1-c
Lt. Raymond K. Wheaton
Sgt. LeLon D. Whitehead
Pfc. John G. Wickwire
Pfc. Robert G. Wilkinson
Cpl. Jack Williams
T-Sgt. Harold Wiseman
Pvt. Michael J. Wojcik
A-C Richard Wolff
Pfc. Lyle M. Wood
Pvt. Pearston Woodward
Raymond F. Worden, HA 1-c
Pfc. William John Wooley
Cpl. Anthony Zeller
Pvt. Lawrence Zuver
Pvt. Anthony Zyckowski

A picket fence surrounds the 1st Marine Division's Cemetery on Okinawa. Most of the graves came from the 1945 battles that resulted in the heaviest American casualties of the Pacific war. The picture was taken during a visit by Army Pfc. Austin Ladd.

Voices of World War II

The "Voices of World War II" DVD features Jackson County people and their experiences during World War II. The interviews are a joint project by Jackson Citizen Patriot writer Bradley Flory and staff photojournalist Dave Weatherwax.

Fred A. Bahlau
Army

Leonard Owczarzak
Army

Russell Bjorkman
Coast Guard

Robert Vance
Army

Maryan (Myron) Czubko
Marine Corps

Stanley Vavryca
Army

Robert Kendall Jr.
Army Air Corps

Clifford "Todd" Weatherwax
Army Air Corps

Philip Leathead
Army Air Corps

Richard Zeller
Marine Corps

Elaine Massey
"Rosie the Riveter"

Leon "Lee" Zimmerman
Army Air Corps

We are deeply indebted to the following who generously shared their treasured photos:

Clinton Abrams
Myrtle Amley
Phyllis Anderson
Bina Arehart
Charles Ahronheim
Stanley Augustine
Fred Bahlau
Joanne Bahlau
Frank Barrett
Malcolm Bater
Harold Bean
Betty Bell
Kathy Bennett
Sherman Berkeypile Jr.
Eleanor Blanchard
Donald Brininstool
Winifred Brockie
Margo Brogan
Delores Brouard
Ruth Broughton
Diane Brush
Phyllis Bungart
Frances Burdick
Teresa Burkey
Tammy Butts
Mike Caldwell
Judi Campbell-Omo
Stephen Casler
Fran Champney
Jean Chmielewski
Cindy Clark
Walter Clark
Donald Cooke
Donna Cox
Bea Crandall
Margaret Culhane
Valda Davidowicz
Chris Davis
Penny Desmoreaux
Warren Dexter
Chuck Dickerson
Donald Douglas
Robert Drongowski
Karen Dunigan
Zoa Edwards
Everett Farr
Philip Farrand
Dolores Field
Janet Finch
J. W. "Jay" Freeman
Melissa Freeman
Karen Fritz
Charlene Gage
Albert Gaige
Brian Garred

Ann Gawlik
Roberta Gebhardt
Linda Gibbs
Ann Gier
Bill Goudie
Lanny Green
Gorson Greening
Steve and Pat Gregerson
Bonnie Haehnle
Laura Haines
Margaret Haitt
Florence Hammond
William Hampton
Sheila Harmon
Evelyn Hartman
Jan Hawkins
Harriet Haystead
Carl Heath
Ellen Hemry
Shelly Hendrick
Ival Hendrick
Earl Hill Sr.
Constance Hobde
Kenneth Hoch
William Hoffman
Dale Hons
Nancy Hopkins
Connie Horning
Jan Houghton
Jane Hudechek
Delaine Hudson
Wendell Huggett
Mary Huntoon
Monica Jenkins
Connie Kearns
Robert Kendall Jr.
Theodore Keyes
Pat King
Kelly Kohn
Philip Kokoczka
Mary Konkol
Doreen Kurtz
Bernard Lacinski
Roger Lake
Stuart Lake
Mary Ann Lapinski
Philip Leathead
Douglas Leffler
Henry Leigh
Lena Leverett
Kay Linden
Scott Linden
Gerald Louagie
Marian Lougheed
Barbara Lubahn

Nick Luppo
Gloria Mahaffey
Thomas Maybourne
Anna Mayer
MaryAnne McAtee
Joseph McCarthy
Shirley McCleer
Judi McCord
John McDermott
Angela Mentink
Carol Metz
Sandie Miller
Lavern Mills
Phyllis Moeckel
Betty Morris
Hugh Morrow
Linda Kurpinski Nabozny
H. Louis Nash
Louis O'Connell
Marilyn Osterhout
Florence Otis
Leonard Owczarzak
Johene Parker
Rozanne Warner Pauze
Tracie Peek
Edward Phelps
Gary Phillips
Margaret Pieron
Jeff Piotrowski
Murray Pond
Pamela Rains
Don Ramirez Jr.
Russell Ratkiewicz
Beverly Reasoner
Mary Reese
Edward "Ted" Reeve
Diane Reynolds
Judy Reynolds
Robert Rice
Gale Richardson
Robert Richardson
Timm Richardson
Elwyn "Rabbit" Rider
Howard Robb
Pat Robins
Ralph Robinson
Judy Rockwell
Angie Ropp
Brenda Ruffing
Barbara Rumler
Kenneth Salsbury
Theresa Schmidt
Pat Schultz
Diane Schweda
Carolann Sherwood

Richard Skrzynski
Margie Slugay
Lorraine Slusser
Allen Smith
Joyce Smith
Virginia Smith
Joyce Smoyer
Claude Spencer
Janice Stetler
Ricky Stoddard
Ken Strickrodt
Thomas Sussex
Jane Swihart
Susan Syrjamaki
Franklin "Jim" Tilford
Barb Torres
Cheryl and Terry True
Anita Trujillo
Harold Tucker
Harry Twardowski
Stanley Vavryca
Dorene Vincent
Teresa Vinton-Zakrzewski
Charles Walker
Karen Walker
Inez Walworth
Delynn Ward
Brian Weber
Lydia Weeks
Barbara Wellman
Robert Wellman
Ruth Wellman
Richard Wendt Jr.
Barbara Whitbeck
Robert Whiting
Marilyn Williamson
Clark Winchell
Elaine Woodworth
Ronald Wyatt
Christina Young
Mary Zaborowski
Richard Zeller
Lee Zimmerman

Special thanks goes to Ella Sharp Museum of Art & History, especially Judy Horn and Ken Schluckebier, and David M. Welihan of Jackson County Veterans Affairs.

Index